The McGraw-Hill 36-Hour Course in Business Writing and Communication

Manage Your Writing®

Kenneth W. Davis

McGraw-Hill

New York   Chicago   San Francisco   Lisbon   London   Madrid   Mexico City
Milan   New Delhi   San Juan   Seoul   Singapore   Sydney   Toronto

The **McGraw·Hill** Companies

Excerpts from *Better Business Writing: A Process Approach* by Davis, © 1990, are reprinted by permission of Pearson Education, Inc., Upper Saddle River, NJ.

Cartoons from the series *The Neighborhood* by Jerry Van Amerongen: © Reprinted with special permission of King Features· Syndicate.

7 8 9 0   DOC/DOC   0 9 8

ISBN 0-07-144127-1

McGraw-Hill books are available at special quantity discounts to use as premiums and sales promotions, or for use in corporate training programs. For more information, please write to the Director of Special Sales, McGraw-Hill Professional, Two Penn Plaza, New York, NY 10121-2298. Or contact your local bookstore.

Library of Congress Cataloging-in-Publication Data

Davis, Ken, 1945-
    The McGraw-Hill 36-hour course in business writing and communication :
    manage your writing / by Kenneth W. Davis.
       p. cm.
    ISBN 0-07-144127-1 (pbk. : alk. paper)
    1. Business writing. 2. Business report writing. 3. Business communication. I. Title:
    McGraw-Hill thirty-six hour course in business writing and communication. II. Title.
    HF5718.3.D38 2005
    651.7'4—dc22

                    2004025896

To Bunny Holman and the memory of Larry Holman
Clients and beloved friends

CONTENTS

Acknowledgments   vii

Introduction: Manage Your Writing   **1**

Be Your Own Communication Department   2
Writing in a Knowledge Economy   6
What a Writing Course Can—and Can't—Do   9
How to Use This Book   11
"The Discipline of the Craft"   12
Managing Your Writing Time   13
The Law of the Next Action   16
The 12 Steps   18
Manage Your Writing   20
Manage Your Writing *Today*   21

1. Find the "We": Manage Your Relationship with Your Reader   **23**

Communication and Community   25
Personality   27
Attitude   29
Circumstances   32
Knowledge   35
Exercise   36
Manage Your Writing *Today*   38

2. Make Holes, Not Drills: Manage with Purpose   **41**

Death to Subject Lines   44
Ko and *Mei* Communication   46
The Long and Short of It   47
The Communication Grid   48
Exercise   51
Manage Your Writing *Today*   53

3. Get Your Stuff Together: Manage Your Information   **55**

Asking Questions   57
Outside and Inside   60
Map Your Information   61
Exercise   63
Manage Your Writing *Today*   65

4. Get Your Ducks in a Row: Manage Your Structure   **67**

An Everyday Example   69
The Technique of Organizing   72
Formulas   73
How to Change Minds   77
From Information to Knowledge   79
Exercises   80
Manage Your Writing *Today*   82

5. Do It Wrong the First Time: Manage Your Drafting   **85**

Draft as Prototype   86
Exercise   88
Debriefing the Exercise   88
Overcoming Writer's Block   89
Writing and "Flow"   90
Manage Your Writing *Today*   92

**6. Take a Break and Change Hats: Manage Your Internal
   Writer and Editor**   **95**

Breaking for Objectivity   95
From Writer-Based to Reader-Based   98
The Two Hats   100
Exercise   104
Manage Your Writing *Today*   106

7. Signal Your Turns: Manage Your Paragraphs   109

Tools for Revision   110
Turn Signals   112
Exercises   118
Manage Your Writing *Today*   121

8. Say What You Mean: Manage Your Subjects and Verbs   123

Hidden Subjects   124
Hidden Verbs   126
Hidden Subjects and Verbs   127
Active or Passive   128
Modifiers   129
Exercises   131
Manage Your Writing *Today*   133

9. Pay by the Word: Manage Your Sentence Economy   135

Objectivity and Common Sense   137
Two Tools   139
Beckwith on Economy   140
Exercises   140
Manage Your Writing *Today*   143

10. Translate into English: Manage Your Word Choices   145

Learning from the IRS   147
Word Histories   149
Good Reasons Otherwise   153
SEC Guidelines   155
Readability Formulas and Style Checkers   156
Deliberate "Obfuscation"?   159
Three Examples   161
Exercises   161
Manage Your Writing *Today*   164

11. Finish the Job: Manage Your Spelling, Punctuation, and Mechanics   167

Exercise   171
Manage Your Writing *Today*   173

12. Manage Your Writing: Evaluate Your Writing Process   **175**

    Manage Your Writing *Today*   175

Appendix A: Manage Your Online Writing   **179**

    The Writing Machine   179
    Four Challenges   181

**Appendix B: Manage Your Global Writing: The Case of the
Belgian French Fries**   **185**

    A Communication Grid   186
    The Global Communicator   187
    Using the Grid   188

Appendix C: Manage Your Speaking   **189**

Appendix D: Resources for Managing Your Writing   **193**

    Books on Communication in Business   193
    Dictionaries   194
    Thesauruses   194
    Usage Guides   194
    Writing Guides   195
    Other Books   195
    Web Resources   196

Answer Key to Exercises   **197**

Index   **205**

Final Examination   **E-1**

ACKNOWLEDGMENTS

For making this book possible, I thank

- My colleagues in the Department of English, Indiana University-Purdue University Indianapolis, especially Christian Kloesel, chair and friend
- My fellow members of the Association for Business Communication, the Association of Professional Communication Consultants, and Dynamic Toastmasters Club
- My past and present students and clients
- My agent, Paul S. Levine
- My designer, Dean Eller, of DesignMark, Inc., Indianapolis
- My team at McGraw-Hill, especially Kelli Christiansen, Stephen Issacs, Janice Race, and Dan Silverburg
- My friends and fellow writers Professor William Hutchings and the Reverend Robert Myers
- My wife and partner, Bette Davis

MANAGE YOUR WRITING

I N THIS KNOWLEDGE economy, writing is the chief value-producing activity. But you may not be writing as well as you could. That may be because you think writing requires a special talent that some people have and some people don't.

In fact, writing is a process that can be managed like any other business process. If you can manage people, money, or time—then you can manage your writing.

And you can profit from the results.

This book will give you the tools to become—in the next 36 hours— a more effective, efficient manager of your own writing.

- You'll become more effective because you will learn to produce writing that gets things done.
- You'll become more efficient because you will learn to produce more effective writing in less time.

How can this magic happen in just 36 hours? It will happen because you will learn to take the management skills you already have and apply them to the process of writing. Remember, whether or not manager is part of your job title, you clearly are a successful manager. Otherwise, you wouldn't have

- the money to buy this book,
- the position to have somebody else buy it for you,
- or the time and initiative to be browsing through it in a bookstore.

Through your experience, in business and in life, you've learned to manage: to manage people, to manage money, to manage time. This book will teach you how to use these same skills when you write.

1

Let me tell you a story. When I was a kid growing up in rural Iowa, there was a local fisherman who had more money than common sense. That is, he always had the newest, most expensive fishing gear, but he didn't always put it to the best use.

One fall he decided to take up ice fishing. He ordered the very best cold-weather clothing, the very best portable shelter, and the very best ice saw and tackle. The first winter day our local reservoir had frozen over enough for safe ice fishing, he was out on the ice at dawn. He set up his shelter, sawed his hole in the ice, sat on his new folding stool, and waited.

Three hours passed without even a sign of a fish. The disgusted fisherman was about to call it quits and head home when he saw a teenage kid in faded blue jeans and a faded green Army field jacket head out onto the ice. The kid whacked a hole in the ice with a hammer, baited a hook, and immediately pulled out a nice fish. Within 10 minutes, the kid had a bucketful and turned back for the shore.

The older man yelled for him, but the kid was apparently out of voice range. So the man started walking fast toward him and finally caught up with him at the shore.

"Son," the man said, "I've been out here three hours without catching a fish, and you've pulled out half a dozen in 10 minutes. What's your secret?"

"Hmrm hmrm," the boy muttered.

"What's that?" asked the man.

"HMRM HMRM," answered the boy, louder.

"I'm sorry, son; I can't understand you. What's your secret?"

The boy moved his hand to his face and took a handful of something out of his mouth.

"WARM WORMS."

Well, OK, that story didn't really happen. But I wanted you to believe, for a while, that it had happened in order to make two points:

1. Writing can change, and even create, reality. For a while, my words made that story real for you. And the writing you do on the job can create a new, better reality for you in your work life.
2. This will be a "warm worms" book. It will give you practical, down-to-earth tools—the equivalent of a hammer, a bucket, or a mouthful of night crawlers—to recreate yourself as a more effective, efficient writer.

BE YOUR OWN COMMUNICATION DEPARTMENT

A *New Yorker* cartoon shows a tiny newsstand with a big sign. "Fred's Newsstand—," it reads, "Forefront of the New Post-Industrial Information Society."

We're all Fred, of course. The information society is a fact, and it affects the work every one of us does, from building cars to selling newspapers. As John Naisbitt has written, "The information society is an economic reality, not an intellectual abstraction." Yet most of us haven't learned the skills we need to survive and thrive in this new knowledge economy.

This fact is particularly important given that more and more of us are entrepreneurs—and "intrapreneurs." For the small business owner—or for the owner of "You, Inc.," within a large business—the upside of the knowledge economy is the fact that the creation or communication of knowledge does not require a large organization; the lone David can compete effectively with the Goliath. For example, some of the computer programming for a London cab company has been done by a lone entrepreneur working from his Indiana farmhouse. The downside, however, is that the same standards of communication excellence are expected from a one- or two-person operation as from a giant corporation with its own communication department.

So how do you compete? By being your own communication department.

Begin by understanding the times we live in. One of the most perceptive commentators on the knowledge economy is Alvin Toffler. His book *The Third Wave* outlines three times of major change in human activity:

1. The first of these "waves," says Toffler, came several thousand years ago when hunting and fishing were replaced by farming as humanity's main work. In the resulting agricultural economy, wealth consisted chiefly of the ownership of land.
2. The second wave happened only about 150 to 200 years ago when farming was replaced by manufacturing as our major economic activity. (That revolution—the industrial revolution—was not a bloodless one: the U.S. Civil War was, to some extent, a conflict between a largely agricultural South and an increasingly industrialized North.) In the resulting industrial economy, wealth consisted chiefly of the ownership of factories.
3. Now, says Toffler, a third wave is sweeping over us. Manufacturing has been giving way rapidly to the processing of information as humanity's major economic activity. As we have entered the information or knowledge economy, wealth has come to consist of the ownership of information—or rather, the ability to collect and communicate information. James Champy is right when he says, in his book *Reengineering Management*, "Knowledge is power, as the cliché has it. But knowledge is not easy to come by. You earn it by thinking. And all we have to think about is information. So make sure that the information 'gets around.'"

As early as the late 1980s, Tom Peters was finding striking examples of the wealth that lies in communicating information. Peters reported that the little publication called *The Official Airline Guide*—a for-sale compilation of schedule information that the airlines gave away free—sold in 1988 for $750 million, three times the selling price of Ozark Airlines that same year.

In other words, the right formula for collecting and communicating free airline information was worth more than all the planes, equipment, and other assets of an airline itself.

If collecting and communicating information is our main work for today and tomorrow, we'd better get good at it. In a knowledge economy, our personal success and the success of our organizations depend on this "knowledge work." Management guru Peter Drucker, writing in *Managing in the Next Century,* puts it this way: "Physical resources no longer provide much of an advantage, nor does skill. Only the productivity of knowledge workers makes a measurable difference."

Unfortunately, however, most of us are not very good at communicating our knowledge, and the results can be disastrous. W. Edwards Deming estimated that "85 percent of failures in quality are failures in communication." A big part of the problem is the way we think about communication. Too often we make third-wave communication decisions as if we were still living in a first- or second-wave society.

In first- and second-wave societies, communication often was one-way, top-down. Information was held at the very top of organizational pyramids and passed down to workers only as needed. Most of the time, most people—whether they worked in a field or in a factory—needed to be only passive receivers of communication.

Moreover, in first- and second-wave societies, communication communities were small and homogeneous. A first-wave farmer may have communicated with only a few hundred people in a lifetime, all people very much like himself. A second-wave plant manager communicated with more people, but that manager probably saw them as interchangeable.

In their book *Thinking for a Living*, Ray Marshall and Marc Tucker point out that our educational system has not yet caught up with the communication needs of a knowledge economy. "Schools' curriculum and methods," they write, "are matched to the needs of a half-century ago, rather than to today's requirements. Fifty years ago, relatively few students needed sophisticated communications skills, so students were not required to write much and teachers were not asked to spend much time working with them to improve what they wrote. Students are still not required to write much and teachers are given very little time to help them improve their writing."

In third-wave organizations, pyramids have been flattened or dissolved, and valuable knowledge resides everywhere. All members of the organization have to be not only consumers of communication but also producers of it. Everyone in a third-wave organization has to be a skilled communicator. As marketing wizard Harry Beckwith writes in *The Invisible*

Touch, "Communication is not a skill. It is *the* skill." And "perhaps the most important lesson from the Iraq war," write David Newkirk and Stuart Crainer, "is that managing real-time communications is as important as managing real-time processes. Communication is moving from being a peripheral, specialist responsibility to being an essential and integral element of corporate leadership." Similarly, central to all five recommendations of the 9/11 Commission was the need for improved communication.

Moreover, a third-wave knowledge worker may well communicate with tens of thousands of people from diverse backgrounds around the world. This diverse audience makes communication much more complex, demanding greater flexibility and sensitivity.

In the knowledge economy, the benefits of improved communication are many. In the insurance industry, for example, the cover letter from the agent, the "producer," to the underwriter is crucial. As Robert Goldstone, vice president and medical director at Pacific Mutual Life, has written, "A good cover letter may save your case." *Forbes* magazine has reported that "at AMEC Offshore, the big British engineering and construction firm, the cost of piping offshore oil platforms dropped 15 percent after intensive work on communications skills." The Families and Work Institute found that "the number one factor employees say will convince them to accept a job offer" is "open communication." And a Watson Wyatt study comparing financially high-performing companies with their lower-performing competitors found that

- "Communications professionals in high-performing organizations play a strategic role."
- "High-performing organizations do a better job of explaining change."
- "High-performing organizations focus on communicating with and educating their employees."
- "High performing organizations provide channels for upward communication."
- "Employees in high-performing organizations have a better understanding of organizational goals and their part in achieving them."

So if you're sold by now—if you're committed to becoming a more effective third-wave communicator—what (besides buying this book) can you do? Here are a few suggestions:

1. Pay attention to the communication you're part of in a typical week. Think about how many messages you receive and send. Consider ways you could benefit yourself or others by communicating more effectively.
2. Pay special attention to the actual results of your speaking and writing. Figure out what communication strategies work for you and

what strategies don't. Notice when you're understood and when you aren't. "There is one thing worse than not communicating," said educational theorist Edgar Dale. "It is thinking you have communicated when you have not."

3. Read and listen to communication from cultures and countries other than your own. In Appendix B of this book you'll learn an approach to communicating across cultures. Meanwhile, however, pick up occasional issues of unfamiliar magazines. Spend a few minutes with a cable channel from another culture or subculture. With each exposure, you'll expand your repertoire of communication techniques.

4. Make sure that your communication process is as efficient and effective as possible. This is what this book is about, of course—streamlining and supercharging your writing process.

5. Start collecting tools—methods and techniques for effective communication. You'll find some especially powerful tools in this book. Also start your own file of effective speaking and writing that you receive. If you get a particularly good direct-mail letter, save it. If you hear a particularly powerful sales presentation, take notes about what's making it so powerful. You'll soon have a useful toolbox of ideas and models.

In short, begin to realize that communication is an important part of whatever work you do. Begin to think of yourself as a third-wave communicator. If you do, you'll be your own communication department.

WRITING IN A KNOWLEDGE ECONOMY

Did you, by any chance, stop to question the first sentence in this introduction? "In this knowledge economy," it claimed, "writing is the chief value-producing activity." This is a pretty big claim—especially when many people think of writing as a skill that's perhaps nice to have but by no means "real work." My former Indiana University colleague, Bobby Knight, spoke for many people when he said, "All of us learn to write in the second grade. Most of us then go on to greater things."

I can't be too critical of Coach Knight. (I wouldn't dare.) Even those people who saw the knowledge economy coming and who realized that knowledge requires communication for it to pay off didn't generally foresee how much of that communication would be in writing.

After all, many messages that a hundred years ago would have been put into writing are now transmitted orally by telephone wire and satellite relay. "Why write a letter," I've been asked, "when you can pick up a telephone?"

This question is an important one. To be sure, oral communication has great advantages:

- First, it can be instantaneous; the moment you decide to say something, you can say it.
- Moreover, oral communication, especially when it is face to face, can carry far more information than mere words can express. A rising pitch or a raised eyebrow can convey shades of meaning not possible on the written page.
- Perhaps most important, oral messages can be answered with immediate feedback, even during the message. You can constantly adjust your communication based on your listener's response.

Speaking, in short, is fast, easy, and efficient.

Writing, in contrast, is almost always slower and more difficult. This is partly because we have much less practice at it. And in a business, writing is expensive, requiring equipment and materials. In addition, the written word, for most of the history of business, has been slow to move, taking hours and days to get from one office, one city, or one nation to another. For all these reasons, the telephone was a godsend to business. Thus, during the late nineteenth century and most of the twentieth century, the proportion of business communication put in writing almost surely decreased.

But oral communication has its disadvantages, too:

- The main one is impermanence. Speech vanishes as soon as it's uttered; this is why an oral contract is "not worth the paper it's written on." Speech can, of course, be recorded, but much of its important content doesn't survive the recording process.
- And even if speech is recorded on tape or disc, its content is extraordinarily difficult to search and retrieve. Try finding every mention of Microsoft in an audio or video recording of a two-day meeting.

Writing, on the other hand, is forever. A written communication can last as long as the material on which it is inscribed, and it is always available for rechecking. This is, in fact, why writing was invented—and for "business" purposes at that. When humanity experienced Toffler's "first wave," moving from hunting and gathering to agriculture, the first writing began to appear, in the form of warehouse inventories and other business documents, on clay tablets. These ancient pieces of business writing are still being found throughout the Middle East.

In her book *Doing Business*, Olivia Vlahos quotes from one of these documents, a clay tablet sent from creditors in the city of Assur, in modern Iraq, to a debtor at the end of a caravan route in modern Turkey: "Thirty years ago you left the city of Assur. You have never made a deposit since, and we have not recovered one shekel of silver from you, but we have never made you feel bad about this. Our tablets have been going to you with caravan after caravan, but no report from you has ever come here. . . . Please do come back right away or deposit the silver for us. If not, we will send you a notice from the local ruler and the police, and thus put you to shame in the assembly of merchants. You will also cease to be one of us."

As Vlahos says, "the modern debt collector would be hard put to better that communication."

The relative permanence of writing also lets it be used to "freeze" oral discussion. Lee Wood, who worked as a writer at Resort Condominiums International, tells of the use of writing there "to give closure, to record agreement." And Terry Pearce, in his acclaimed book *Leading Out Loud*, points out the importance of writing as a way of "disciplining your voice" in preparation for oral communication. "Writing," he says, "reveals fuzzy thinking, exposes slurred distinctions: it clarifies."

In addition to its permanence, written communication has the advantage of being easily skimmed or indexed so that a reader can find exactly that part of the message that she needs. For this reason, many digital audio and video recordings are now accompanied by "written" meta-information: the index of tracks on an audio CD or "chapters" on a DVD, for example. Some CD-ROM products index, in writing, audio or video material down to the level of individual words so that you can, in fact, find every time the word *Microsoft* was spoken during a two-day meeting.

Moreover, the old gap between speech and writing in speed and cost has essentially closed. Computers, networks, and satellite data transmission have made a written message as cheap and fast as a phone call while retaining all the advantages of written words. In addition, the globalization of business, requiring communication across many time zones, has made phone conversations exceedingly inconvenient.

As a result, the century-long trend toward spoken communication has reversed. More and more business communication is being conducted in writing. E-mail and Web pages are, after all, written documents produced to be read. A 2000 study by the Poynter Institute found that readers of online news sites look first at the text—a very different way of reading than in print media, where readers tend to look first at graphics. On the Web, only 22 percent of users look at graphics first.

At the time I'm writing this introduction, the latest use of writing in business is in the form of *blogs,* Web logs of links and other information that can provide crucial just-in-time information to a company's employees or wider stakeholders. *Fast Company* magazine has reported the use of blogs by (predictably) Microsoft and Verizon, as well as (perhaps less predictably) DaimlerChrysler, Hartford Financial Services Group, and IBM.

WHAT A WRITING COURSE CAN—AND CAN'T—DO

Now for a confession—one that's not often made in business writing books: Books and courses about writing can't teach you everything you need to be an effective writer. That's the bad news. But here's the good news: what this book can't teach, you almost certainly already know.

You see, writing involves two abilities. Only one can be taught. If you have the first ability, this book can teach you the second.

The first ability, the one that can't be taught, is what writing teacher and researcher Stephen Krashen calls "competence." Competence is our deep, unconscious knowledge of language. We acquire competence in spoken language by hearing it over and over again. We learn how a language sounds.

For example, can you state the rule in the English language for the order of adjectives of number, age, and nationality? You probably didn't even know there was such a rule; you certainly weren't taught it in school. Nevertheless, you know the rule perfectly. You know to say "two old Japanese accountants," not "old two Japanese accountants" or "Japanese two old accountants." This rule—not really a rule but a practice—is part of your competence in English, learned from hearing and reading thousands of sentences in which this practice was followed.

The English language has tens or hundreds of thousands of such practices, only a few of which ever get taught formally in classrooms and training rooms. Many of these practices—including the example in the last paragraph—apply both in speaking and in writing. Many others, however, apply only in written English. Writing demands an explicitness, a clarity, a degree of organization that speaking does not, and so it requires additional competence. We learn such competence through reading. We learn how writing "sounds."

This reading doesn't have to be great literature. *Sports Illustrated, Scientific American,* or a Stephen King novel will serve as well as Shakespeare. The only requirement is that there be a lot of it and that it be self-motivated. For reading to produce writing competence, it must be *transparent.* The reader must be paying attention not to the words and sentences themselves but to what they say.

By the time you're reading this book, you almost surely have the competence you need to be an effective business writer. But don't stop. To continue to grow as a writer, you need to continue to grow as a reader. As the American novelist William Faulkner said, "Read, read, read. Read everything—trash, classics, good and bad, and see how they do it. Just like a carpenter who works as an apprentice and studies the master. Read! You'll absorb it. Then write."

What teaching or training can do is take writers who already have competence and give them a second ability, an ability that Krashen calls "performance." Performance is the ability to actually produce language.

Performance always lags behind competence. Any parent knows that children have competence in spoken language (they can understand it) long before they acquire performance (and start talking).

Almost any child who grows up around English speakers will soon learn to translate his competence into spoken performance. But performance in writing is more difficult to achieve. And that's where teaching and training come in. For adults, training (like the course in this book) can give those who already have competence in written English three important components of performance.

1. Confidence

The first component that training can provide is confidence. One of the main reasons that the writing performance of most adults doesn't match their competence is that they lack confidence in their ability to write. They are consciously or unconsciously afraid of failing. *Writer's block* is perhaps the most familiar symptom of this lack of confidence.

So this book, like all good writing training, is attitude-based. It will help you to realize the competence you already have and remind you that writing is much more than just following rules. As the beginning of this introduction said, this book will stress the fact that writing well is not a talent that you are either born with or not; it is a business activity that can be competently managed like any other business activity.

2. Process Knowledge

The second component that training can provide is process knowledge. The knowledge about writing that comes from extensive reading is all product knowledge. Just as you can drive cars for years without having any idea about the automobile manufacturing process, you can read books and articles for years without having any idea about the writing process—the false starts, stumbles, and revisions that writers have to go through. Jonathan Swift, author of *Gulliver's Travels,* described the process this way:

> *Blot out, correct, insert, refine,*
> *Enlarge, diminish, interline;*
> *Be mindful, when invention fails,*
> *To scratch your head, and bite your nails.*

Therefore, this book, like all good writing training, is process-oriented. Rather than focusing on details of written products, such as clauses and colons, it focuses on the steps good writers go through, the decisions they make. This is why the best writing teachers and trainers are also working writers, "walking their talk."

3. Reinforcement

The third component that training provides is ongoing reinforcement. Some of this reinforcement can be in the form of reminders of the attitudes and process knowledge that writers have learned in their training. Some can be in the form of feedback, responses to work in progress.

This book offers four opportunities for reinforcement:

1. Most chapters have exercises for you to complete, then compare your answers with mine.
2. The book ends with an examination leading to a certificate of completion.
3. The book includes lots of advice on how to evaluate yourself and how to learn from the feedback you get on your on-the-job writing.
4. You can go to my Web site, www.ManageYourWriting.com, and subscribe to a free weekly e-mail tip, called "Manage Your Writing This Week," that will give ongoing reinforcement of what you've learned in this book.

The three components of effective writing training—confidence, process knowledge, and reinforcement—are interdependent. As you become more confident, you'll become more receptive to new process knowledge and more willing to seek and receive feedback about your writing. As you gain more process knowledge, you'll become more confident about your writing process and more skillful at receiving reinforcement. And as you receive (and give) ongoing reinforcement, both your confidence and your process knowledge will grow.

Training in writing can't do everything. But with the competence you already have, this book can make you more confident and knowledgeable—and thus more efficient and effective. And it can make you a lifelong learner of writing, getting better and better each day, week, month, and year.

HOW TO USE THIS BOOK

This book has 12 chapters, or lessons, each covering a step in an effective writing process.

As I've mentioned, most chapters have exercises to complete. Most also ask you to apply what you've learned in that chapter to the very next piece of on-the-job writing you do—and evaluate the result. Including exercises, on-the-job applications, and self-evaluations, the 12 chapters should take you an average of three hours each to complete.

This book also includes four appendices:

- Appendix A, "Manage Your Online Writing," deals with special considerations for writing for online reading: e-mail, Web pages, blogs, and the like.
- Appendix B, "Manage Your Global Writing," gives you some special tools to use when you write internationally.
- Appendix C, "Manage Your Speaking," tells you how to use what you've learned in this book when you make oral presentations.
- Appendix D, "Resources for Writers," lists further tools.

As you work through this book and after you've finished, please feel free to e-mail me at ken@ManageYourWriting.com and to visit my Web site at http://www.ManageYourWriting.com.

Let me repeat what you've read earlier:

In this knowledge economy, writing is the chief value-producing activity. But you may not be writing as well as you could. That may be because you think writing requires a special talent that some people have and some people don't.

In fact, writing is a process that can be managed, like any other business process. If you can manage people, money, or time—then you can manage your writing.

And you can profit from the results.

"THE DISCIPLINE OF THE CRAFT"

In a cartoon I saw once, a Hollywood producer summons his secretary. "I want to send a memo to the parking-lot attendant," he bellows. "Get me a couple of writers."

Indeed, writing is not often easy or fun, and those of us in business are usually too busy to give it the time that it *seems* to demand. Even people like me who list "writer" as a profession on our 1040 Forms often wish we had staff writers on call to handle those difficult letters, memos, and e-mails that seem to pile up.

However, most of us—even in large organizations—have to do what this introduction has already said: be our own communication department. We have to take personal responsibility for the stream of writing tasks that crosses our physical and virtual desktops.

This is probably as it should be. As designer, "information architect," and entrepreneur Richard Saul Wurman says, "You shortchange yourself if you think that writing is 'someone else's problem.' . . . Even if your job description says nothing about writing, by regarding yourself as a writer, even privately, you can take advantage of the discipline of the craft."

This quotation is wonderful for two words in particular and for its overall message:

- One key word is *discipline.* Writing certainly is a discipline—in the sense that chemistry is a discipline or yoga is a discipline—and like them, it requires discipline. As Larry Gelbart, creator of the *M*A*S*H* TV series, has said, "How to begin a writing project? Put your ass down in your chair, and hope that your head gets the message." Fortunately, the rest of this introduction will show you how to make that discipline a lot less painful.

- The other key word in Wurman's quotation is *craft.* A craft is something that lies somewhere between an art and a science. A good potter, for example, needs both an eye for beauty and a knowledge of the chemistry and physics of clay. Similarly, a good writer needs both an "ear" for the language (the competence discussed earlier) and a knowledge of what makes an effective and efficient writing process.

- And Wurman's overall message is important because as a teacher and trainer, I've seen over and over again that people become what they call themselves. A young person who thinks of himself as a failure may well fulfill that prophecy. A young person who thinks of herself as a success may well succeed. One university writing teacher I know has her students sign their essays not in the usual place at the top but at the bottom, followed by a comma and the word *Writer.* She believes, as Wurman and I do, that "regarding yourself as a writer, even privately" lets you "take advantage of the discipline of the craft."

As this introduction has already suggested, what probably keeps most of us from regarding ourselves as writers is the belief that the ability to write well is a talent or a gift. For some, it surely is: the great novelist, poet, or playwright is doubtless born as much as made. But the everyday business writing that you and I do—the writing that gets the world's work done—requires no special gift. As researcher Frank Smith says, "it is a mistake to regard the thinking that underlies writing as something special, as a unique kind of activity that calls for unusual efforts and abilities."

MANAGING YOUR WRITING TIME

Managing writing is largely a matter of managing time. Writing is a process, occurring over time, and like any process, it can be done efficiently or inefficiently. Unfortunately, most of us have a pretty inefficient writing process.

This is so because we try to get each word, each sentence, right the first time. Given a letter to write, we begin with the first sentence. *"What do I want to say? I'll try a word or two. Is this sentence going to work? Maybe not. Better backspace and start again. Another word, then another. Better. A third word. Spelled correctly? Better check. OK, go on. A verb. Agree with subject? What next?"* And so it goes, word by word, sentence by sentence, through the letter. In an hour of writing, as shown in Figure I-1, we might spend five minutes this way on each of a dozen sentences.

An Eastern Washington University research survey reported that "ineffective writers revise and plan almost entirely in the context of the individual sentence." "For the ineffective writer," the study continued, "drafting proceeds as a linear production of single sentences that typically adds up to a first-and-final draft."

This is like building a house by starting with the front door—planning, building, finishing it, even washing the little window in it—before even breaking ground for the rest of the building. No wonder most of us have so much trouble writing.

Efficient, effective writers take better charge of their writing time; they *manage* their writing. Like homebuilders, they spend time planning before they start construction, and once they're into construction, they don't try to do all the finishing touches—such as washing the windows—as they go.

Many good writers break their writing process into three main stages—*planning*, *drafting*, and *revising*—with more time spent at the first and third stages than at the second. Communication consultant Lee Clark Johns, in her excellent book, *The Writing Coach*, reports a study of one professional writer who spent his writing time this way:

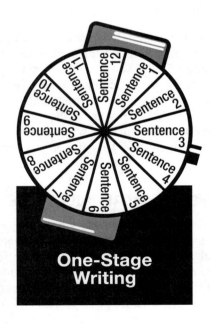

FIGURE I-1   One-stage writing.

- 40 percent "prewriting" (planning)
- 20 percent "writing" (drafting)
- 40 percent "rewriting" (revising)

Many good writers also build in some *management* time at the beginning and the end of the process, and some *break* time in the middle.

OK, so now we have a plan. *Personnel Journal* has reported that the average business letter or memo takes 54 minutes to write, so let's round that up to an hour. As shown in Figure I-2, let's (somewhat arbitrarily) assign time this way:

- 20 minutes of that hour to planning
- 5 minutes to drafting
- 25 minutes to revising

Let's build in a five-minute break between drafting and revising and call the remaining five minutes *managing,* splitting it between the beginning and end of the hour. Rather than spending five minutes on each of a dozen sentences, we'll spend each five minutes doing some very specific managing, planning, drafting, "breaking," or revising work.

FIGURE I-2 Five-stage writing.

And that will be the basis for this course. As we move through the 12 chapters of this book, we'll be moving through the 12 five-minute segments of a typical writing hour. For each segment, you'll learn some very specific, very practical, "warm worms" tools to use at that point in your writing process. By the end of this 36-hour course, you'll have an efficient, effective method for doing on-the-job writing, and you'll have a toolbox of powerful tools to use along the way.

Incidentally, as you circle the clock face for each writing job, you'll be tracing what Joseph Campbell called the "monomyth," the journey of the hero or heroine

- from the "real" world of home,
- into a hidden underworld where he or she slays dragons or passes some other test,
- and then back into the real world with gifts or benefits.

As you move through the writing process, you'll

- start in the real world around you, planning how to address a problem in that world,
- then descend into the private, hidden world of drafting,
- and then gradually return to the real world as you revise to meet the needs of your audience.

Do it well, and you'll be a heroine or hero. This book will show you how.

THE LAW OF THE NEXT ACTION

There's one more powerful advantage of five-stage writing—especially when it's further divided into the 12 steps that are the basis for this book. As Fergus O'Connell writes in his strategy book, *The Competitive Advantage of Common Sense*, "To do anything requires a sequence of events. Knowing this gives you the skills to plan, prioritize, accelerate projects, and get many things done at the same time."

I call this the *law of the next action.* This concept comes from David Allen's book, *Getting Things Done: The Art of Stress-Free Productivity*, one of my top-five most useful business resources. The heart of Allen's work-management method is determining, for each of your projects, the next physical action.

As Allen points out, you can't really "do" a project, such as buy a new DVD player, for example. What you *can* do is determine the next action, such as look up Ruthann's number so that you can call her and ask where she got the great DVD deal that she was talking about. Many projects in our lives look overly daunting, get repeatedly postponed, and cause us a lot of anxiety in the process because we haven't thought about, and written down, what the next physical action is. For example, using Allen's method, I currently have a list of 19 active projects—low for me because I've put so many projects on inactive status so that I could focus on the single project of writing this book—and I've listed the next physical action required for each of them.

Those active projects no longer haunt me any more than my inactive ones do for two reasons:

- They're written down outside my head.
- Whenever I want a break from writing this book, I can move forward on any of the other 18 projects simply by taking the next physical action.

I don't carry the law of the next action as far as Susan does in Figure I-3 (and David Allen assures me that he doesn't either). Like Susan, however, I've learned the value of building workdays around a series of short-term goals—that eventually add up to long-term results.

This is what the five-stage, 12-step writing process model does: It takes what is often the scary job of writing a document and breaks it into a

FIGURE I-3   Susan's days are built upon a series of short-term goals.

series of next actions. You don't have to think of yourself sitting down and spending an hour writing a letter. You just have to spend a couple of minutes on the first "next action": *managing* the time you'll take to do the letter. After you've done that, you can go do something else if you want or need to—because you know that all you have to do next on the letter is the first five-minute task in the planning stage. And so on.

Author John Gregory Dunne, who should know, has written that "writing is manual labor of the mind: a job, like laying pipe." Exactly. Nobody can lay a pipeline. All you can do is lay the next length of pipe. And even eating an elephant is easy if you do it a spoonful at a time.

THE 12 STEPS

Enough background. Now that you know why we're going to divide the writing process into 12 steps, you need to know what they are.

At the *managing* stage (perhaps 2 or 3 minutes for a one-hour writing job), remind yourself that you're a writer, that writing can be managed, and that it's largely a matter of managing time. Therefore, start with 12 on the clock, as shown in Figure I-4. Plan your next hour—remembering that if you choose, you can spread it over several hours, days, or even weeks.

FIGURE I-4   Manage your writing.

At the *planning* stage (perhaps 20 minutes for a one-hour writing job):

1. *Find the "we."* Define the community to which you and your reader belong. Decide how you and your reader are alike and different in personality, attitude, circumstances, and knowledge. Chapter 1 will give you tools for making this decision.
2. *Make holes, not drills.* This is what a consultant once told a major tool manufacturer. That is, focus on the outcome you want, not the means you'll use to achieve it. Define your purpose. Chapter 2 will show you how.
3. *Get your stuff together.* Collect the information you'll use in your writing. You'll get some help in Chapter 3.
4. *Get your ducks in a row.* Organize your information so that you can give it to your reader in the most useful order. Chapter 4 will give you some good organizational strategies.

At the *drafting* stage (perhaps 5 minutes for a one-hour job):

5. *Do it wrong the first time.* Do a "quick and dirty draft" without editing. You'll learn why and how in Chapter 5.

At the *break* stage (perhaps another 5 minutes):

6. *Take a break and change hats.* Get away from your draft, even if for only a few minutes, and come back with a fresh perspective—your reader's perspective. Chapter 6 will provide some tips for making the most of the break.

At the *revising* stage (perhaps 25 minutes):

7. *Signal your turns.* Just as if you were driving the lead vehicle in a convoy, you're leading your reader through new territory. Use "turn signals" to guide your reader from sentence to sentence. Chapter 7 will teach you this especially powerful tool.
8. *Say what you mean.* Put the point of your sentences in the subjects and verbs. Don't worry, Chapter 8 will remind you how to recognize subjects and verbs and show you how their effective use can strengthen your message.
9. *Pay by the word.* Make your sentences economical. You'll learn tools for doing so in Chapter 9.
10. *Translate into English.* Keep your words simple. (Lee Iacocca put steps 9 and 10 in one "commandment of good management": "Say it in English and keep it short.") Chapter 10 will be your translation guide.

11. *Finish the job.* Check your spelling, punctuation, and mechanics. You'll get a quick refresher course in Chapter 11.

Finally, at the *managing* stage again (2 to 3 minutes):

12. *Manage your writing.* Evaluate the process you've just finished. Figure out how to improve it next time. You'll get help from Chapter 12.

Notice that these 12 steps take the same amount of time as the "one-stage" sentence-by-sentence method that many ordinary writers use. In fact, most people who have learned this method tell me that by managing their writing process, they're able to write faster. But even if you don't write faster, you'll be able to write more efficiently and effectively. You'll be able to use your writing to make good things happen for you and your organization. As writer Margaret Atwood says, "A word after a word after a word is power."

MANAGE YOUR WRITING

That's all there is to it. If you quit the course at this point, you'll have already received maybe half its value. You've already learned three important lessons:

1. Writing is a process that can be managed.
2. Writing tasks should not be tackled all at once but in stages.
3. More time should be spent in the planning and revising stages than in the drafting stage.

The rest of this book consists of learning specific tools to use at these stages.

You also know already what to do in the first two or three minutes of a typical writing hour:

■ Remind yourself that you're a writer and that writing can be managed.
■ Allocate time for the 12 steps of the writing process.

Completing this important step will make you not only a better manager of your writing but also a better manager of everything else: people, projects, money, time. In their book *What They Really Teach You at the Harvard Business School*, Francis J. Kelly and Heather Mayfield Kelly point out that "too often, we make major communications decisions without thinking them through at all. Or we just say or write whatever first comes to mind. . . . There are always choices to be made. The most effective managers will make them quickly, but also wisely."

MANAGE YOUR WRITING *TODAY*

Start with the very next writing job you have to do. Instead of diving right in and working on the first sentence, stop for a couple minutes and do some writing management: Remind yourself that you're a writer, that writing can be managed, and that it's largely a matter of managing time. Then set up blocks of time for planning, drafting, and revising—with more time allocated for planning and revising than for drafting. Give yourself at least one break, between the drafting and revising stages.

When you've finished the writing job, take a few minutes to evaluate how the process worked for you. Don't worry if writing this way seemed awkward or unproductive at first; we all have a lot of old habits to replace. With practice and time, you'll become a much more effective and efficient writer.

1

FIND THE "WE"

MANAGE YOUR RELATIONSHIP WITH YOUR READER

PEAKER JOE GRIFFITH tells a story of the FBI under J. Edgar Hoover: "A young FBI man was put in charge of the FBI's supply department. In an effort to cut cost, he reduced the size of memo paper.

"One of the new memo sheets ended up on J. Edgar Hoover's desk. He disliked it immediately and wrote on the narrow margin, 'Watch the borders.'

"His message was misinterpreted. For the next six weeks, it was extremely difficult to enter the United States by road from either Mexico or Canada."

Such misunderstandings happen all the time in organizations large and small. Most result from poor planning. You'll recall that in the introduction I divided the writing process into five stages: managing, planning, drafting, breaking, and revising—and then back to managing again. This chapter begins with the planning stage, a stage that should take perhaps 20 minutes of a typical writing hour.

You may be a one-stage writer, used to starting your writing process by immediately drafting and revising the first sentence of your document. If so, you may be afraid or suspicious of postponing drafting for as long as 20 minutes out of an hour. You may be saying, "I can't afford to spend a third of my writing time without actually *writing* the thing." As communication consultant Lee Clark Johns comments, "People often say, 'I don't have time to plan.'" "But," says Lee, "if you want to become a reader-friendly writer, you don't have time *not* to plan."

I agree absolutely. Remember the old business saying: "To fail to plan is to plan to fail."

As shown in Figure 1-1, you begin the planning stage with the five-minute step I call "Find the 'We.'" This step is about defining the main relationship in which any piece of writing exists: the relationship between writer(s) and reader(s). This relationship needs to be defined before any other meaningful decisions can be made. Jay Sidhu, chief executive officer (CEO) of Sovereign Bank, says it this way: "Communication is in the mind of the recipient: you're just making noise if the other person doesn't hear you."

Several decades ago, when the United States and the USSR were planning their first joint space mission, planners thought long and hard about how the language barrier would be crossed, especially in the kinds of perilous situations that could occur in early space flight. Naturally, the American astronauts were taught Russian, and the Soviet cosmonauts were taught English. But which language should be used when and by whom?

The answer may surprise you. After extensive study, NASA announced that the U.S. crew would always speak Russian, and the Soviet crew would always speak English. Why? Because the speaker, who knew what he wanted

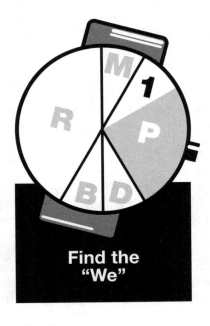

FIGURE 1-1   Find the "we."

to say, could most easily do the work of mental translation. With lives at stake, the listener should not have to *both* mentally translate *and* absorb new information.

This principle applies to everything we write, even to speakers of our own language. We know what we want to say, so we bear the burden of making our message as easy as possible for our reader to understand.

A helpful term that has entered common business vocabulary in the last decade or two is *internal customer.* This is a helpful term, if only because it reminds writers that they have to treat every reader as a *customer.* In fact, Tom Peters argues that everyone in business, even an employee of a large company, should think of herself as a professional service firm with an array of clients or customers. And while the customer may not always be right, it's important to treat customers as if they are. We need to make it as easy and as stress-free as possible for the customer to do business with us. Oliver E. Nelson, Jr., account executive at Energy Systems Group, taught me what I've begun to think of as "Nelson's golden rule": "Write unto others as you would have them write unto you."

To follow this rule, we first need to understand our customer—our reader.

COMMUNICATION AND COMMUNITY

Most of us in business have heard the advice to make our communication not *I*-centered but *you*-centered. Most business writing textbooks, including ones that I've written, tell us to focus not on the sender but on the receiver. They tell us to write not "I will send you a check" but "You will receive a check."

This advice is good. But it's not good enough. It's based on an incomplete model of the communication process, a model that can be diagrammed as in Figure 1-2.

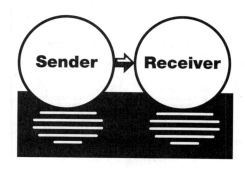

FIGURE 1-2   The sender-receiver model.

But this model and the advice based on it ignore the fact that we in business are never isolated writers or speakers communicating with isolated readers or listeners. We communicate within organizations—ideally within communities. The relationship between sender and receiver always has to be thought of in a larger context, as shown in Figure 1-3. As Peter Drucker says in his classic book, *Management*, "There can be no communication if it is conceived as going from the 'I' to the 'Thou.' Communication works only from one member of 'us' to another."

It's no accident that the words *communication* and *community* both come from the same Indo-European roots: *ko* and *mei* (pronounced "may"), meaning "together" and "change." (My company, Komei, Inc., is named after this fact.) A community is a group of people who "change together." Communication is what allows communities to change and what keeps them together *as* they change.

Native American cultures traditionally have known that community is necessary for communication to happen. Thomas W. Cooper writes that for Native peoples, "Without genuine communion [another "ko-mei" word], there could be no meaningful communication. Thus the entire communication ethic was firmly based on spiritual communion."

But communication is not only necessary to community, it also *creates* community. If the quotation in the preceding paragraph was uncomfortably mystical for you, consider this one by dollars-and-cents reengineering guru James Champy: "It is authentic communication that brings people together into a community—listening, responding, confronting, asserting, and disputing—engaged in the perpetual process of change."

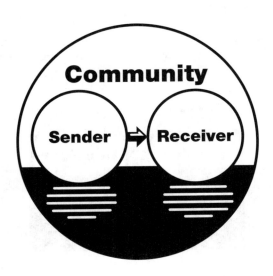

FIGURE 1-3   The community model.

So the best business communication is not just *I*-centered or *you*-centered—it is *we*-centered. To make our e-mails, letters, and reports more we-centered, we need to ask two questions.

The first is, "To what community do my reader(s) and I both belong?" Are we members of the same department or division within an organization? Are we fellow shareholders of the same company? Are we members of the same profession? In short, what makes us *us*?

Try to find the smallest meaningful community that answers this question. The newspaper *USA Today* has enjoyed great success with its "we" approach, although sometimes it has been ridiculed for making its community too big. When we read headlines like "We're Eating More Kelp," all us non-kelp-eaters suddenly feel left out of the *USA Today* community.

To ask, "What is the smallest community my reader and I are both part of?" is to ask a very practical "warm worms" question. You'll find that if you define this community at the very beginning of the writing process, all kinds of other decisions will fall into place for you. Difficult pieces of writing suddenly will become easier if instead of focusing on the antagonisms or differences between you and your reader(s), you focus on the community you're both part of, on the similarities that exist. Even if you're angry at your reader(s) and have a complaint about your readers' performance, you'll find that you can frame your message in the context of what you both want to happen—larger market share, say, or better work environment.

Lee Wood, former writer for Resort Condominiums International, says, "Writing is always an extension of the relationship you have with a person." She notes that such a focus is especially important now, with so many organizations experiencing great change.

Some writers find it helpful at this step in the process to draw a circle on a piece of scratch paper. Label it with the name of the community you share with your audience. Then around that circle draw circles for any larger communities of secondary audience members. Will a memo for your team, for example, also be read by higher management outside the team? (Remember that often you have a secondary audience that exists only in the future, when someone takes advantage of the relative permanence of writing to check what you are writing in the present.)

Add to the diagram an arrow to represent your communication. Are you bringing information into the community from outside? Are you taking information the other direction, from inside out? Are you moving information from point to point within the community? You can use your sketch as a visual aid throughout the rest of your writing process.

PERSONALITY

The second important question to ask at this step is, "Within this community, how are my reader(s) and I alike and different?" Specifically, consider how you and your reader(s) are alike and different in four ways: *personality,* *a*ttitude, *c*ircumstances, and *k*nowledge. To remember them, think of the acronym *PACK* as you "pack" for your journey around the clock face through the rest of the writing process.

The first dimension in which to consider similarities and differences is personality. The most used way of categorizing personality is the Myers-Briggs Type Indicator (MBTI) employed in many organizations. The MBTI measures personality on four scales:

- *Extroversion (E) or introversion (I)*—roughly whether one draws energy from other people (E) or from within oneself (I).
- *Sensing (S) or intuition (N)*—roughly whether one draws information from the senses (S) or from intuition (N).
- *Thinking (T) or feeling (F)*—roughly whether one makes decisions based on logic (T) or on emotions (F).
- *Judgment (J) or perception (P)*—roughly whether one sets priorities rationally or spontaneously.

Together, these four variables produce 16 combinations or *types.* Although certain professions tend to attract certain types, this tendency is by no means absolute. A professional colleague of mine, an Air Force major who worked at the War College, once told me that among generals and admirals in the U.S. armed forces, all 16 MBTI types are represented.

If you know your MBTI type and those of your readers, you're especially fortunate: You'll be able to answer the "personality" question with great precision. If you know only your own type and can make a decent guess about those of your readers, you'll still be able to do excellent planning. Even if you've never heard of MBTI, however, your general people skills will allow you to make very good decisions at this step—and you'll be able to understand much of the following advice, based on the research of communication consultant Dan Dieterich:

- If you're an extrovert, you may need to get all your thoughts on paper very early; you may, in fact, "think by writing." Thus you may want to write a very rough draft as part of step 3 and then reorganize it in step 4 so that you'll be able to write a much more organized draft in step 5. When you write to introverts, be sure to build community. Be careful not to overwhelm them with your position.
- If you're an introvert, you may find it hard to move out of the planning stage into "quick and dirty" drafting. You'll be helped by this book's advice, in step 5, about drafting without editing. When you write to extroverts, try to overcome your reticence by projecting self-assurance.

- If you're a sensor, be sure to move beyond the specific details in your writing to generalizations or conclusions. Be careful about trying to apply writing "rules" too rigidly; realize that you need to adapt to your specific writing situation. Make sure that you postpone your concern with spelling, punctuation, and mechanics until step 11, where it belongs. When you write to intuitives, focus on your main point or points, not on details.
- If you're an intuitive, make sure, at step 3, to gather a thorough list of facts and specific details. When writing to sensors, make sure to include enough details to support your main point or points.
- If you're a thinker, be sure to pay attention to the next section of this chapter, "Attitude." When writing to feelers, show empathy.
- If you're a feeler, you may need to be more structured and less sentimental. Pay special attention to step 4 of the writing process. When writing to thinkers, make your message clear and logical.
- If you're a judger, you may rush into the drafting stage without enough careful planning. When you revise your drafts, make sure that you thoroughly "change hats" from writer to reader in step 6. When writing to perceivers, be sure to be flexible. (Incidentally, as a judger, you'll naturally embrace the five-stage, 12-step method outlined in this book, but you'll need to keep reminding yourself that every situation is different and that flexibility is important.)
- If you're a perceiver, you may need to focus on your purpose and be concise. Give special attention to step 2 in the planning stage and step 9 in the revising stage. When writing to judging types, don't be afraid to come to a conclusion and express it forcefully. (Incidentally, as a perceiver, you may find this book's five-stage, 12-step method rigid and difficult, but practicing it, at least for a while, will give your writing process some needed structure. Then you should feel free to modify it to suit your own personality.)

ATTITUDE

A number of years ago, when I was writing another business writing book, I was listening to one of my favorite radio programs as I worked. The program host, a skilled writer in his own right, spoke a short sentence about writing that was absolutely perfect for the chapter I was writing. So I immediately jotted it down.

The sentence was short enough that I knew I could legally and ethically quote it in my book—giving the host credit, of course—without getting his permission. But because I had only heard, not read, the sentence, I wanted to give the host a chance to see what I was planning to say and a chance to correct or revise the sentence if he wished. So I wrote him a letter. And because I was a real fan of his show, I turned it into a fan letter as well as an informational letter. After giving him the chance to revise the quotation, I spent the rest of about two pages talking about the things I especially liked about the show and comparing it to some programs I had listened to as a child.

In a couple of weeks, I got back a two-sentence letter, not from the host but from a member of his production staff:

_____ Public Radio

Dear Mr. Davis:

We are flattered that you wish to include part of _____'s monologue in the textbook that you are writing, but it is Mr. _____'s policy not to give out the text of his _____ monologues. The main purpose behind our show is entertainment, as you well know, and we do not feel that it would make appropriate teaching materials.

Yours truly,

_____

I was ticked off—not because the host wouldn't confirm the quotation. I knew I could legally and ethically use the sentence anyway. I was annoyed that the writer of the letter was condescendingly telling me how to do my job. Who was this person to tell me what would make "appropriate teaching materials"? I'm a textbook writer; she's a radio producer. I hadn't told her how to do *her* job!

And I also was annoyed that the "fan letter" content of my letter hadn't even been acknowledged.

Now don't get me wrong. I don't think at all that the writer of the letter meant to insult me. I suspect, instead, that she was a one-stage writer with a pile of mail to answer. She didn't take the time to consider her relationship with me—and as always, not to decide is to decide. If she had thought about it, she would have realized that my public radio station would twice a year be asking me for money—in part to support her show. If she had thought about our attitudes, hers and mine (hers: rushed; mine: supportive and eager), she wouldn't have unnecessarily alienated me. She would have left out the judgmental language about textbooks and the snippiness of "as you well know." And she would have added a brief response to my radio reminiscences and an acknowledgment that while she couldn't confirm the quotation, she realized that I was free to use it anyway.

You see, all of us come to everything we write and read as people, with feelings and attitudes. Too often, as business writers, we forget all that, thinking of ourselves and our readers not as people but as profit centers or boxes on a line-and-block chart.

Instead, as you begin a writing job, ask what feelings about this communication you and your audience share. What feelings don't you share?

Some writing and speaking is like paddling downstream with the current of your audience's attitudes; some is like paddling upstream against the current. Businessman Donald Walton writes, "Keep in mind at all times that nobody (except you) cares a hoot about what *you* want. The people you're writing to care only about what will be good for them. You have to figure out carefully what that is, and then tell them about it. If you do that consistently, they'll like you. Also, they'll think you're smart. Because you are."

One good tool to use in assessing your readers' attitudes is to ask what need your writing will be filling for them. As you may know, according to psychologist Abraham Maslow, all human beings have the same basic needs that they strive to satisfy. These needs are arranged, says Maslow, in a hierarchy, as shown in Figure 1-4. The needs at the bottom of Maslow's "pyramid" come first, but as they are satisfied, "higher" needs emerge.

Ask yourself which of these needs your piece of writing will satisfy for your audience. By way of illustration, consider the story that entrepreneur Peter Hay tells about men's clothing tycoon Max Hart. According to Hay, Hart "summoned his advertising manager to complain about his latest campaign: 'Nobody reads that much copy,' he asserted.

"The ad manager begged to differ. 'I'll bet you ten dollars, Mr. Hart, that I can write a whole newspaper page of solid type, and you will read every word of it.' Hart eagerly accepted the bet.

"'I won't have to write even a paragraph to prove my point,' the ad man continued. 'I'll just give you the heading:

"This Page Is All About Max Hart.'"

FIGURE 1-4   Maslow's hierarchy of needs.

The advertising manager had clearly diagnosed that his boss (like other people whose lower-level needs have been met) had a need for self-esteem and the esteem of others. The proposed heading was targeted directly at that need.

But whether or not you consciously use Maslow's hierarchy of needs, if you invest, at the planning stage, even a few seconds of time in considering your reader's attitudes, your writing is guaranteed to be more effective. As advertising legend David Ogilvy wrote, "The most effective leader is the one who satisfies the psychological needs of his followers."

CIRCUMSTANCES

Several times in my career I have heard a story—probably apocryphal—about the testing of a new fighter plane. According to the story, the Air Force had contracted for a new fighter. The manufacturer had produced several prototypes to flight-test before full production could begin.

Everything was going smoothly until suddenly a problem arose. A test pilot had radioed in that he was bailing out, but didn't, and was killed in the crash. Flight tests, of course, stopped until it could be discovered what was wrong with the ejection system.

On the ground, everything seemed to work correctly. But in the air, something had gone wrong. Finally, the Air Force and the manufacturer called in an outside consultant. The consultant arrived at the test site, climbed into the cockpit of one of the planes, and had the canopy lowered over him.

He noticed that on the canopy, just to his left, were the instructions for ejection: three easy steps. "Step 1: Pull the red lever below to release the canopy."

Some of you will already have seen the problem. On the ground, you pull the red lever, and the canopy unlocks but just sits there. In the air, you pull the red lever, and—WHOOSH!—the canopy is a mile behind you, along with instruction steps 2 and 3.

Fortunately, most of us aren't in the business of giving life-and-death instructions. But even in many seemingly routine messages, we need to consider the circumstances in which the reader will be receiving our communication. If the communication is face to face, the circumstances are obvious: the room, the lighting, the acoustics, the time of day. However the circumstances of a written communication are just as important. For example, consider this memo from one of my clients, a Fortune 100 company. I've changed only department names and numbers.

> In order to have effective controls on automobile repairs and to insure proper and prompt payment of invoices, all repairs and purchase of tires for automobiles will be administered by Motor Pool, Department 680, effective

March 1. Prior to taking your automobile to a vendor for work, contact Motor Pool, extension 6729, to obtain a purchase order and release. Complete a blanket purchase order release form with Department 680 as department ordering and price is to be marked advise, complete account code and department charge, then obtain buyer's signature.

Upon completion of form give a copy to the vendor when you take the vehicle in for the service. After the work has been completed check the bill to insure there are no arithmetic or extension discrepancies and verify that sales tax has not been included. On the bill state that service has been received, then have two signatures on the bill with the purchase order and release order number. When the invoice is correct and approved, send it to Motor Pool for processing.

If you have any questions, please contact me. Thanks for your assistance in this matter.

This memo went out to perhaps a thousand employees of a single plant. I was shown it six months later because it simply hadn't worked. Most employees simply weren't following the directions.

You don't need me to tell you what was wrong. The memo is wordy, hiding crucial steps in the middle of long paragraphs instead of displaying them openly in a numbered list. And a lot of sentence-level revisions are needed.

The biggest problem, however, is in the planning stage—specifically in a failure by the writer to consider the circumstances in which employees would be reading the memo. I asked the company representative, "On the day the memo was received, how many employees needed repairs or tires for a company car and so could use the information that very day?" The answer was very few, probably just 2 or 3. For the remaining 997 or so, the memo had no immediate use, so it was trashed or buried in a file cabinet. Three or six months later, when one of those 997 employees needed tires or car repairs, he or she may well have forgotten even receiving the memo, much less what it said.

My advice to the company representative was to consider the circumstances the readers would be in and not send a memo at all. Instead, I recommended that the company revise the form to make it self-instructional, put a pad of these forms in the glove compartment of each company car, and put a small sticker on the dashboard that said, "Need repairs or tires? Use the form in the glove compartment."

I can't claim a win on this one. The company didn't follow my advice. But I hope that the people I talked with became more aware that writing is never read in the abstract. It is always read in very specific circumstances.

Marketers, perhaps more than any other businesspeople, truly understand the importance of considering audience circumstances. According to David Graulich, on the public radio show "Marketplace," a small disk-drive manufacturer, during a gigantic Las Vegas computer trade show, "arranged to have Las Vegas cab drivers ask their passengers, 'Do you know who makes the fastest disk drives?' If an employee of the manufacturer was in the cab when the driver asked the question, the cabbie got paid one hundred dollars. The company says it got a terrific response, with lots of people calling up to ask about the product, or to argue about whether their disk drive really was the fastest." The point? The manufacturer's marketers realized that at the trade show, a cab ride offered a rare "captive" situation, a distraction-free circumstance in which to get a marketing message through.

So at step 1, in your planning stage, spend at least a few seconds thinking about the circumstances in which your message will be read. Imagine your reader not just as a face (like the passport-style photos in some contact-manager programs) but as a complete person at a particular place and time. Ask yourself, will your message be the only piece of business writing your reader will receive this week, or will it be one of a hundred e-mails competing for your reader's attention tomorrow morning? As writers Herbert E. Meyer and Jill M. Meyer put it, "A piece of writing gets one shot."

So picture your reader as he receives and reads your message. If you're lucky (or unlucky) enough to have a reader like the one shown in Figure 1-5, that's how to imagine him.

FIGURE 1-5   Whether one enjoys reading reports has a lot to do with *how* one reads them.

Follow the advice of famed sports agent Mark H. McCormack: "Most people are so engrossed in the message they are trying to convey that they forget to step out of themselves and think about the reader. The most effective communicators try to visualize the person reading and reacting to their writing."

So give it a try. The more you can imagine the reader's circumstances, the richer, clearer picture you'll have of your reader, and the more effective your writing will be.

KNOWLEDGE

The fourth and last dimension in which to consider how you are like and unlike your reader(s) is knowledge. Whenever you write something to a reader, the two of you have to have some knowledge in common, or communication isn't possible. To be part of the necessary community, you have to share some knowledge.

However, there also has to be some knowledge you don't have in common. If you and your reader already share total knowledge of the subject, communication isn't necessary. As I've gotten older, I've learned why older married couples don't always talk a lot with each other. It's not because they are bored with each other or because they've run out of things to say. It's because in many situations they already know what each other is thinking. Normally in business, though, you don't have that level of intimacy. There's a knowledge gap somewhere—and it's that gap that much business writing is designed to bridge.

Some years ago a manager at one of my client companies shared a feedback form the company had received about one of its software manuals. In the manual, the writer had felt a need to define the term *default value*.

As you may know, a default value is a preset variable. In Microsoft Word, for example, the default value for the left margin is 1.25 inches. If you want 1.0 inch or 1.5 or 2.0 inches instead, you can easily ask for them. If you don't ask, you get 1.25.

The writer of the manual had been more creative than that. The manual defined *default value* by analogy. It said, suppose that you stop at the same coffee shop on your way to work every morning, and you almost always order a doughnut and a cup of coffee. Soon that becomes your "usual"—your default value for breakfast. Even if you just grunt, they'll bring you a doughnut and coffee. If on some days you ask for a muffin instead, you'll get it. But unless you do that often, a doughnut remains the default value.

That manual, with its explanation of default values, found its way to Japan. A Japanese employee of the company filled out the feedback form at the end of the manual and returned it to company headquarters in the United States. The form read

Sorry inconvenience your time. Concerning explanation of you in page 95 "Default values" I have difficulty explaining to my customer what is a doughnut and what is a muffin. Can you send me both each? How is it shown in listing?

Thankfully,

_____

And then a signature, in Japanese characters. Now I'm confident that the feedback form was written for humorous effect, a way of pulling the corporate leg. I think the use of "Japanese English" was a part of the joke. But whether the feedback was serious or not, it makes an important point. If you're trying to explain default values by comparing them to doughnuts and muffins, you'd better make sure that your audience knows what doughnuts and muffins are. If not, you've made your message less clear.

We all have our own "doughnuts" and "muffins." Whether our audience is across the world or across the hall, we all have words and concepts whose meaning is obvious to us but will not necessarily be obvious to our audience. Technical writers and editors have an acronym, *COIK,* that stands for "Clear Only If Known." You'll sometimes find that an editor has scribbled "COIK" beside a passage that will be perfectly clear to any reader who already shares the writer's knowledge (and thus doesn't need to read the passage in the first place) but not at all clear to a reader who doesn't share that knowledge.

If the COIK material consists of just a technical term here and there, it can be corrected in the revising stage. However, eliminating COIK material often involves substantial rewriting. For this reason and others, therefore, it's more efficient to avoid COIK material in the first place by making consideration of your audience's knowledge an important part of step 1, "Find the 'We,'" at the planning stage.

Incidentally, if you do write for audiences around the world—and more and more of us in business do—Appendix B, "Manage Your Global Writing," will give you a framework for more effective international business communication.

_____

EXERCISE

The following questions will test your understanding of this chapter. The final examination for this course will include similar questions.

1. Why is defining your community—your relationship with your reader(s)—the first step in the planning stage?

   a. It comes first alphabetically.

    b. It is represented by the *P* in the acronym *PACK.*

    c. All other planning decisions depend on it.

    d. It is the most difficult step.

2. Which of the following statements is most true?

    a. Community is necessary for communication.

    b. Communication is necessary for community.

    c. Both *a* and *b* are true.

    d. Neither *a* nor *b* is true.

3. In defining the community to which you and your reader(s) both belong, which of the following communities should you focus on?

    a. The largest possible community

    b. The smallest possible community

    c. The corporate community

    d. The international community

4. In thinking about your audience, which of the following questions should you ask?

    a. How are my audience and I alike?

    b. How are my audience and I different?

    c. Both *a* and *b.*

    d. Neither *a* nor *b.*

5. When you and your reader(s) have different personality types, which of the following best expresses what you should do?

    a. Simply be yourself, in the confidence that your reader(s) will be able to adjust.

    b. Consider both your personality type and those of your readers, and adjust as necessary to your readers' personalities.

    c. Ignore personality differences; they are unimportant in business communication.

    d. Find common ground with your reader(s) in a third personality type.

6. If you're a "feeler" writing to a "thinker," which of the following should you do?

    a. Avoid being overly sentimental.

    b. Make sure that you support your opinions logically.

    c. Make your thinking process clear.

    d. All of the above.

7. Which of the following statements about attitudes is most true?

   a. Similarities and differences between your attitude and that of your audience should be considered at the planning stage.

   b. Consideration of similarities and differences between your attitude and that of your audience should be postponed until the revision stage.

   c. Consideration of attitudes should not enter into the business writing process.

   d. None of the above.

8. Which of the following statements about the Maslow hierarchy of needs is most true?

   a. It is a handy checklist of punctuation rules.

   b. It can help you to assess how your writing can fill a need for your reader(s).

   c. It describes the five needed stages in the writing process.

   d. None of the above.

9. In visualizing your reader(s), which of the following statements is most true?

   a. You should visualize your reader(s) at their best.

   b. You should visualize your reader(s) at their worst.

   c. You should visualize your reader(s) reading and reacting to your message.

   d. You should focus on your reader's face.

10. Which of the following best expresses the meaning of the acronym *COIK?*

   a. COIK material will be understandable by the reader(s) only if they already know it.

   b. COIK material is adjusted to the four elements of the personality of your reader(s).

   c. COIK material considers circumstances, opportunities, intelligence, and knowledge of your reader(s).

   d. None of the above.

MANAGE YOUR WRITING *TODAY*

Now that you've checked your understanding of Chapter 1, you should put it into practice right away.

- On the very next writing job you have to do, begin with some writing management: Remind yourself that you're a writer, that writing can be managed, and that it's largely a matter of managing time. Set up blocks of time for planning, drafting, and revising—with more time allocated for planning and revising than for drafting.

- Then begin the planning stage by "finding the 'we.'" Take perhaps five minutes to ask yourself, "What is the smallest community to which my audience and I both belong?" and "How are my audience and I alike and different in the four PACK dimensions: personality, attitude, circumstances, and knowledge?" Answer these questions very explicitly this first time, making notes about your answers.
- Now go ahead and do the rest of your planning, thinking about purpose, content, and organization. (You'll learn specific planning methods in the next three chapters.)
- Then draft your document with as little editing as possible.
- Take a break.
- Then revise it.

When you've finished the writing job, take a few minutes to evaluate how the process worked for you. Evaluate especially whether "finding the 'we'" resulted in a more effective message at the end.

2

MAKE HOLES, NOT DRILLS
MANAGE WITH PURPOSE

ACCORDING TO BUSINESS legend, a large tool manufacturer once called in a consulting team to look at the company's whole operation, from drawing board to packing case. At the exit interview, the lead consultant addressed the tool company's executives. "Ladies and gentlemen," he said, "the most important thing you need to remember is that you're not in the business of making drills. You're in the business of making holes."

The consultant probably meant two things. First, he was stressing the importance of knowing what business you're really in. In nineteenth-century America, the railroad companies were wealthy and powerful beyond imagination. If you had asked one of the railroad barons what business he was in, he would have said "the railroad business." Wrong answer. He would have been thinking much too narrowly. If, instead, those powerful railroad companies had thought of themselves as being in the transportation business, they might have survived and ended up owning airlines, trucking firms, and overnight express companies. Similarly, the consultant was telling the tool manufacturer that it should define itself broadly. If a technology comes along to replace the drill (lasers, perhaps?), the company should be prepared to dump drill-making and move on.

This is important advice. But more important to us as business writers is the second thing that consultant probably meant. He meant that it's crucial to know the *purpose* of what you're doing. If you focus on just making drills, it will be too easy to forget why your customer wants to buy a drill in the first place. Some major tool manufacturers truly have learned this lesson: they give away dozens of free project plans in order to give their customers reasons to drill holes.

Most of us business writers haven't learned this lesson. If a coworker interrupts us while we're writing a letter and asks, "What are you doing?" most of us will answer, "Writing a letter." This is focusing on the piece of writing—the tool—itself, not on its purpose. The result: Our writing often misses the chance to be as effective. At this crucial second step of the planning stage of the writing process, shown in Figure 2-1, don't ask yourself about the document you're going to write. Instead, ask yourself what effect you want to have on your reader(s). If a coworker interrupts your writing and asks what you're doing, be prepared to answer, "I'm trying to make this customer forgive us for the shipping mistake we made."

For example, a common mistake in writing job application letters is the failure to understand their purpose. Most job application letters should not be written for the purpose of getting a job but for the purpose of getting an interview. Getting the purpose right will help you to get on the interview list.

Thomas W. Cooper has written that Native American chief, actor, and activist Dan George "never spoke without a reason. . . . What was more important than George's words was that such words were born only of purpose. He had a purpose for silence, and a purpose for speaking." We should

**Make Holes,
Not Drills**

FIGURE 2-1 Make holes, not drills.

learn from this. We should learn not to speak or write until we have a clear sense of why we're speaking or writing. Instead, we're too often like Jason in Figure 2-2, "strong on 'How' and weak on 'Why.'"

Oliver E. Nelson, Jr., of Energy Systems Group, says that "knowing what your purpose is not only makes the document better; it helps remove ego problems—because then you know what your job is, to get something done, not to make yourself look better."

Sports agent Mark McCormack has written that "business memos usually have two purposes—either to project your ideas onto the company or to protect you from other people's ideas. Make your choice before you write a word. Whether you're advancing your cause or defending your turf, your readers won't be clear about it unless you are." Although I don't find McCormack's two choices particularly helpful, I love his advice: Your readers won't be clear about your purpose unless you are.

This is our task for this five-minute segment of a typical writing hour. We need to be very clear about what we want. We've managed our writing process, and we've found the "we" by identifying the community that we share with our audience and the ways in which we and our audience are alike and different. Now it's time to focus on what we want—specifically on what we want our reader(s) to know or do as a result of reading our message. We need

FIGURE 2-2 Jason is strong on "how" and weak on "why."

to remember Vincent McHugh's advice that "self-expression is for babies and seals, where it can be charming. A writer's business is to affect the reader."

In short, we need to focus on holes, not drills.

DEATH TO SUBJECT LINES

Some years ago a life insurance company got a new young chief executive officer (CEO) from a human resources (HR) background. Almost immediately he became concerned about the poor quality of memos coming across his desk. (This was, incidentally, in the very first year or two of e-mail, so most memos were still being written on paper.) The problem with these memos wasn't misspelling or incorrect punctuation or bad grammar; it was an overall lack of focus and clarity, making them difficult to get through. He asked me to work with him to turn the problem around. He wanted his company to be known as the best communicator in the business.

His first impulse, and mine, was to do massive training. But we remembered what psychologist Abraham Maslow (you'll remember him from Chapter 1) said: "If all you have is a hammer, everything looks like a nail." Therefore, instead of diving into training, we had a series of meetings with the CEO's team of senior vice presidents. Although we did end up doing some training, the most important thing we did was redesign the company's memo form.

The first problem with the old form was its heading: "Interoffice Correspondence." If you start to write on a form that begins "Interoffice Correspondence," you get the subliminal message that you are supposed to do wordy, stuffy, pretentious writing (more about that in Chapter 10). So we gave our new form the simple heading "Memo."

The next things on the old form were "Date," "To," and "From." Fair enough. We left those alone. But the next line read "Subject," just as in 99 percent of the memos and 100 percent of the e-mail messages you've read. It's a feature of memos that began when file folders and file cabinets were introduced into business (before then, correspondence was done by hand and copied into large ledgers). Subject lines weren't invented for writers and readers but for file clerks. And subject lines positively invite vagueness. As one of my trainees once told me, "The hardest thing about writing memos is filling in the subject. So you just throw something in there. When the reader gets it, it's the part he or she reads first. And the subject line may not be what you want them to get out of it."

Therefore, we killed the subject line on the memo form.

However, we didn't eliminate the subject line until we had found a good replacement for it. Our memo form had a new line: "Purpose." And to help the writer, we made the answer multiple-choice. Below "Purpose" we put two other lines, each with a check box before it:

Purpose:

☐ to tell you about _____.

☐ to ask you to _____.

The writer checks either or both of these purposes and fills in the blank or blanks.

For the writer, the new form demands that the "hole," not just the "drill," be considered right at the beginning of the writing process. If the writer of the memo about automobile tires and repairs in Chapter 1 had used this memo form, he might have checked both purposes and written:

Purpose:

☑ to tell you about <u>the new auto-repair policy.</u>

☑ to ask you to <u>do the following steps when you need repairs or tires.</u>

The obvious advantage of this purpose line was for the reader. When you get a memo on the new form, you know right up front whether you're just being told *about* something or being asked to *do* something. You can decide immediately whether to read the rest of the memo or set it aside for now or forever. If you read it, you can read it with the purpose in mind.

Management consultant Bill Jensen wrote in his book *Simplicity*, "About 80 percent of your internal communication—meetings, teleconferences, presentations, emails, etc.—consists of

- Sharing information that does not require action, and/or
- Communicating something for which there is no discernible consequence if the recipient ignores it

"In other words, a lot of communication you thought was helpful may be seen as unfocused noise or just 'FYI' junk mail by your teammates." The new memo form allowed readers to screen out "noise" immediately. It allowed readers to ask immediately WIIFM?—"What's In It For Me?"

However, the bigger advantage of the purpose line was for the writer. Having to think about your purpose at the beginning almost guarantees that your writing will be more effective. So whether or not you actually begin labeling your subject lines as purpose lines, do take five minutes or so at the beginning of planning any message by asking yourself, "What is my purpose: to tell my audience about something or to ask them to do something or both?"

Shortly after we designed the memo form, Mark McCormack's *What They* Still *Don't Teach You in Harvard Business School* appeared with its list of the eight "toughest" messages to deliver: "(1) This is how you do it. (2) I want to sell you. (3) I goofed. (4) I have some bad news for you. (5) You did a great job. (6) Dear Boss, you're wrong. (7) This is my demand. (8) This is how you rate."

McCormack continues, "I would read a memo that began with any one of these sentences."

KO AND *MEI* COMMUNICATION

"It's not *what* she said; it's *how* she said it." "His *actions* are so loud, I can't hear what he's *saying*." "She *talked* a lot, but she didn't *say* anything."

Comments such as these describe perhaps the most common kind of communication failure: the failure to balance the two main functions of communication. This failure can be largely avoided at this first step of the planning stage of the writing process. To communicate effectively, we need to find the balance.

As discussed in Chapter 1, the word *communication* comes from the Indo-European roots *ko* and *mei* (pronounced "may"), meaning "together" and "change." Some communication takes place primarily for the *ko* function of building or maintaining relationships, of keeping a community *together*. For example, greetings exchanged with coworkers, such as "Hello" and "How are you?" have almost exclusively a *ko* function. (If you want to test whether "How are you?" has a *ko* function, try answering the question honestly the next time someone asks it.)

Other communication takes place primarily for the *mei* function of changing something, of getting something done. For example, a faxed order for a pepperoni pizza (no anchovies, please) probably has exclusively a *mei* function.

Of course, most acts of communication have both functions. When we speak or write, we usually want both to maintain a relationship and to get something done. If you ask a coworker, "Tony, if you don't mind, would you please bring the first-quarter sales figures to the meeting?" you are trying to get the sales figures, but you are also trying to keep on good terms with Tony. Phrasing your request as a question and including the words "if you don't mind" and "please" reveal your *ko* purpose.

The use of such *ko* language by European-Americans interestingly led to a change in Native American communication. Thomas W. Cooper writes, "It is somewhat ironic that the misrepresentative symbol of Native communication—a chief raising his open hand and saying 'How'—was in response to the white man's influence on the Native. The indigenous vocabulary did not include 'How.' But, since the settler and the soldier asked the Native so many questions—'How are you doing?' 'How is your family?' 'How are your crops?' 'How is your health?'—the Native sought to nullify this lengthy examination with one simple 'How?'"

Language experts have used a number of labels for what I call the *ko* and *mei* functions of communication: *social* and *practical, identity-focused* and *task-focused, relationship-oriented* and *content-oriented,* and *interactional* and *transactional.* Deborah Tannen, in such books as *You Just Don't Understand,* refers to these functions as the "meta-message" and the "message" and argues that women and men sometimes value them differently.

But to be effective in an organization, whether you're a woman or a man, you have to balance the *ko* and *mei* functions in what you say and write. To check your balance, ask yourself these questions:

1. Is my communication relationship-oriented or more content-oriented? That is, do I tend to emphasize the *ko* function of togetherness or the *mei* function of change, of action, of getting things done?
2. If I am chiefly a *ko* communicator, how can I become more confident, more assertive, and more willing to ask for a change in other people's actions or opinions?
3. If I am chiefly a *mei* communicator, how can I become less abrupt, more supportive, more sensitive, and more willing to postpone immediate results for the sake of ongoing *relationships*?

THE LONG AND SHORT OF IT

American business is often criticized for its "short-termism." Fairly or unfairly, U.S. executives, boards of directors, and shareholders are charged with obsessive attention to the current quarter's numbers at the expense of longer-term growth. We all seem to be victims of a "what have you done for me lately?" syndrome. Whether or not this is a fair rap overall, it's certainly true of communication. In the talking and writing we do, most of us tend to focus on immediate short-term effects rather than long-term effects. We tend to speak or write for today or tomorrow, not for next year or next decade. To be more effective in business, we need to change this. We need to master long-term as well as short-term communication.

To understand the difference between long-term and short-term communications, let's consider how communication functions in living systems. All living systems, from single cells to the global ecosystem, share certain characteristics. Some of these characteristics have to do with how systems process information—how they communicate. In fact, communication is one of the things that make a system a system, not just a random collection of parts.

In her book, *Leadership and the New Science*, Margaret J. Wheatley discusses this fact:

For a system to remain alive, for the universe to move onward, information must be continually generated. If there is nothing new, or if the information that exists merely confirms what is, then the result will be death. Isolated systems wind down and decay, victims of the law of entropy. The fuel of life is new information—novelty—ordered into new structures. We need to have information coursing through our systems, disturbing the peace, imbuing everything it touches with new life.

Consider the living cell. In a cell, some information is long term, stored in the cell's DNA. As the cell reproduces, this information is communicated from generation to generation. The molecules that make up the cell may change, but this long-term information remains relatively constant. By contrast, some information in a cell is short term, in the form of electrical or chemical "messages," sent within the cell and between the cell and its environment. For example, such a message might carry information about temperature changes.

In an organization, too, some information is long term, relatively permanent, allowing the organization to preserve its identity even as its members come and go. James Moore, writing in *Fast Company* magazine, asked, "What is organizational DNA? It's the stuff, mostly intangible, that determines the basic character of a business. It's bred from the founders, saturates early employees, and often shapes behavior long after the pioneers have passed on." By contrast, some information in an organization is short term, relatively temporary, allowing the organization to stay responsive and alive. To check your balance between long- and short-term communication, ask yourself these three questions:

1. Is my communication more short term or long term in its focus? That is, do I tend to communicate in order to build immediate relationships and get immediate results, or do I tend to ignore immediate goals and take a longer view?
2. If I am a short-term communicator, how can I get a longer-term perspective? How can I start thinking more about long-term effects of my communication?
3. If I am a long-term communicator, how can I focus more closely on the immediate relationships and short-term results that I need in order to realize my long-term goals and visions?

THE COMMUNICATION GRID

The two ways we've discussed of dividing communication—*ko* and *mei* and long term and short term—can be graphed in a matrix, or grid, as shown in Figure 2-3, resulting in four different kinds of communication.

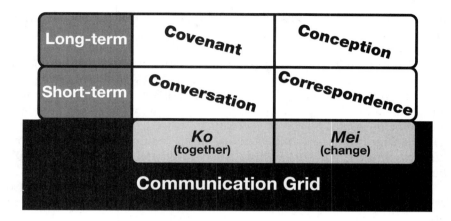

FIGURE 2-3   The communication grid.

The lower-left cell of the grid contains communication that is relatively short term and that has, as its main function, the *ko* function of creating or maintaining community. When you say "Hi" to a coworker, you're operating in this cell of the grid. I call this kind of communication *conversation,* although actual conversation usually has both *ko* and *mei* functions. In his book, *The Postmodern Organization,* William Bergquist argues eloquently for the importance of conversation in an organization. "Goods and machines," he writes, "are *parts* of the organization, whereas *conversations* are the essence of the organization."

This kind of "conversation" can be written as well as spoken. A letter to a supplier that begins "I certainly enjoyed our conversation yesterday; it was fascinating to hear about your trip to Kyrgyzstan," is a letter that begins with "conversation." In fact, for reasons mentioned in the introduction to this book, more and more conversation is occurring in writing, especially in the form of e-mail.

Tom Peters devoted a full chapter of his book *Liberation Management* to CNN as a model of the new organization—Peters would say "disorganization"—required by these fast-changing times. His most striking snapshot is one taken in the early morning as several dozen executives and staffers in Atlanta and elsewhere conduct their daily scheduling meeting, refining a 30-page schedule document that has been drafted the night before. The atmosphere is casual, almost chaotic. Peters writes that during the meeting he observed, most participants "were simultaneously reading newspapers. Side conversations were rife. The chatter was open, free and easy—consistent with the overriding emphasis on action."

Out of this apparent chaos, however, comes a document that literally redefines CNN with each new day. In this company without rigid hierarchies, the daily schedule establishes and reestablishes the shape of the organization. "It's only a minor exaggeration," writes Peters, "to say that the document *is* the network."

Think about that. To say that an organization is created by communication—as noted in Chapter 1—is to say nothing new. Like any living system, an organization is held together by the information that flows back and forth among its components. But to say that an organization *is*, in fact, a document—a piece of business writing—is to say something very new. This is why I'm so committed to speaking, training, and writing about business writing. Business writing is more important today than ever. It's because writing literally *constitutes* the new organization.

The lower-right cell of the grid contains communication that is also relatively short term but that has as its main function the *mei* function of effecting change, of making something happen. Such communication is a kind of "correspondence," although, of course, it includes not only many letters, memos, and e-mail messages but also much oral communication as well. Courses and books on business communication traditionally have emphasized this cell to the exclusion of the other three. In this book, I am trying to remedy that problem.

The upper-left cell of the grid contains communication that is relatively long term and that exists primarily for *ko* purposes. This communication is called *covenant*. Covenant communication includes such documents as mission statements or values statements; it also includes the oral traditions of an organization—its myths and legends. All these forms of covenant communication have the effect of establishing and maintaining the long-term relationships among the members of the organization or between the organization and its various stakeholders. Jack Hawley, in his book *Reawakening the Spirit in Work*, writes that "the leader's first task is to define reality, to make sense of the organization and its environment. As a leader . . . you're signer of a sacred covenant."

In recent years, one kind of covenant communication, the mission statement, has gotten a bad rap. Dilbert creator Scott Adams, for example, has defined a mission statement as "a long awkward sentence that demonstrates management's inability to think clearly." "All good companies," says Adams, "have one." I myself was part of a group that helped an organization define a mission statement for itself, only to hear several months later about a fruitless two-hour search by two employees to find a copy of it. The lesson, of course, is that mission statements, like other forms of covenant communication, have to be living documents, continually communicated in many ways, spoken and written.

For example, in 1990, while planning a video teleconference, I was referred to a person who was described to me as a "keeper of the corporate culture" at Apple. On a formal line-and-block chart, that person wouldn't have been especially prominent, but in the ongoing covenant communication of the company, he played a major role.

The upper-right cell of the grid contains communication that is also relatively long term but that exists primarily for the *mei* function of change. Such communication can be called *conception*. Conception communication includes vision statements, conceptions of what the organization ought to be changing *toward*.

You may be thinking, "What does this all have to do with me? I don't write mission, values, or mission statements everyday." The point, however, is that even when you think of yourself as engaged just in *correspondence*, you'll be more effective at it if you consider your organization's needs for *conversation, covenant,* and *conception* communication as well.

EXERCISE

The following questions will test your understanding of this chapter. The final examination for this course will include similar questions.

1. Why is defining your purpose the second step in the planning stage?

    a. It should be done after defining your community—writer and reader(s).

    b. It should be done before collecting and organizing the content of your message.

    c. Both *a* and *b* are true.

    d. Neither *a* nor *b* is true.

2. Why do subject lines in memos and e-mail messages cause problems?

    a. They weren't invented for the reader(s) of the message.

    b. They are often vague.

    c. Both *a* and *b* are true.

    d. Neither *a* nor *b* is true.

3. Using the subject line to define the message's purpose benefits whom?

    a. The writer, because it encourages the writer to define her purpose

    b. The reader, because it allows him to better screen and read the message

    c. Both the writer and the reader

    d. Neither the writer nor the reader

4. Readers always want to know WIIFM. What do these letters stand for?

    a. Words, images, ideas, format, and mechanics

    b. What's in it for me?

    c. Whether included information facilitates metaphors

    d. Neither *a, b,* nor *c*

5. All communication has both *ko* and *mei* functions. What do these root words mean?

   a. Oral and written

   b. Long term and short term

   c. Communication and community

   d. Together and change

6. Most pieces of communication have what function?

   a. A community-building function

   b. A change function

   c. Both *a* and *b*

   d. Neither *a* nor *b*

7. Which of the following is probably *not* an example of "conversation" communication, as defined in this book?

   a. A birthday card

   b. A discussion, over lunch, of your children's activities

   c. A corporate mission statement

   d. A question about the reader's family at the beginning of a business e-mail message

8. Which of the following is probably *not* an example of "correspondence" communication, as defined in this book?

   a. A birthday card

   b. A telephone call to order office supplies

   c. An e-mail message to order office supplies

   d. A faxed order for office supplies

9. Which of the following is probably *not* an example of "covenant" communication, as defined in this book?

   a. A mission statement

   b. An oral story of your company's founding

   c. A corporate privacy policy

   d. A profit-and-loss statement for the month

10. Which of the following is probably *not* an example of "conception" communication, as defined in this book?

   a. A speech by a CEO projecting five-year goals for the company

b. A corporate vision statement

c. A corporate history

d. A written timeline of goals for the next 10 years

MANAGE YOUR WRITING *TODAY*

Now that you've checked your understanding of Chapter 2, you should put it into practice right away.

- On the very next writing job you have to do, begin with some writing management: Remind yourself that you are a writer, that writing can be managed, and that it is largely a matter of managing time. Set up blocks of time for planning, drafting, and revising—with more time allocated for planning and revising than for drafting.

- Then begin the planning stage by "finding the 'we.'" Take perhaps five minutes to ask yourself, "What is the smallest community to which my audience and I both belong?" and "How are my audience and I alike and different in the four PACK dimensions: personality, attitude, circumstances, and knowledge?"

- Then practice what you've learned in this chapter, taking perhaps five minutes to define the purpose of this piece of writing. Ask yourself, "Is my purpose to tell my reader(s) about something, ask my reader(s) to do something, or both? Will this piece of writing function as conversation, correspondence, covenant, or conception—or some combination of those?" Answer these questions very explicitly this first time, making notes about your answers.

- Now go ahead and do the rest of your planning, thinking about content and organization. (You'll learn specific planning methods in the next two chapters.)

- Then draft your document with as little editing as possible.

- Take a break.

- Then revise it.

When you've finished the writing job, take a few minutes to evaluate how the process worked for you. Evaluate especially whether "making holes, not drills," focusing on your purpose, resulted in a more effective message at the end.

3

GET YOUR STUFF TOGETHER
MANAGE YOUR INFORMATION

SURELY IT'S HAPPENED to you. You've bought something that needs assembling—a swing set, a ceiling fan, or a bookcase. An hour's work, tops. But the instructions are badly written, so you don't read them all. Instead, you just start working. Soon you discover that you need a tool or part that you don't have, so work stops while you make a trip to a hardware store. An hour later you're back on the job, and it happens again. Again, you stop work to go buy what you need. The one-hour job stretches into three or four hours.

I suspect that this has happened to you because it has happened to me. And it happens to most of us when we write. As one-stage writers, we jump into writing memos and letters without making sure that we have the materials—the information—that we need. We get halfway into the first paragraph and realize that we need a number from Alice in Accounting, so we stop to call her. In the third paragraph we remember that we need a product description from an online catalog, so we open a Web browser and find it. As a result of such interruptions, the job takes longer, and the writing is less effective.

If we built houses this way, we'd buy our nails in one little rack package of two or three dozen nails at a time. When we used up each package, we'd stop work to go buy another package. Fortunately, real builders don't work this way. They buy their nails by the box or keg, and they try to buy enough for the job before they start driving nails into boards.

This is what we need to do as writers. As much as possible, we need to collect the information we need before we start drafting. Because the decision about what information to include depends on decisions made about your reader(s) and your purpose, collecting information is the third five-minute step in the planning stage of a typical writing hour, as shown in Figure 3-1.

Collecting information as a separate step before you draft has at least four payoffs for you:

1. It reduces interruptions while you're drafting, giving your draft more continuity.
2. It gives you a chance to focus, for a while, *just* on your information. Such focus is crucial, especially if your information includes facts. Executive Donald Walton, in his book *Are You Communicating?*, says that "the biggest mistake you can make in a report, letter, proposal, or other important message (and it's made all the time) is to write without first getting and correctly analyzing all the facts. It's the one unforgivable mistake. Your boss or customer can overlook a slip in grammar, but not bad advice that results when factual preparation is sloppy and incomplete."
3. It reduces the possibility of omitting important facts or ideas. Unless we systematically capture the facts and ideas we need, they

FIGURE 3-1   Get your stuff together.

can, as shown in Figure 3-2, easily fall off the conveyer belt of our writing process.

4. It gives you the confidence to draft more easily, with much less anxiety. As long ago as the third century B.C., the Roman statesman Cato the Elder wrote, "Get a grasp on your subject and the words will follow."

ASKING QUESTIONS

The key to getting your stuff together lies in the advice given by Warren Bennis and Burt Nanus in their excellent book on leadership, *Leaders: The Strategies for Taking Charge*: "Successful leaders, we have found, are great askers, and they do pay attention."

One "great asker" was Ben Duffy, former head of the advertising agency Batten, Barton, Durstine and Osborn. According to businessman Peter Hay, Duffy, "landed his largest accounts by putting himself into the client's position." Once when Duffy was preparing for a meeting with American Tobacco Company President Vincent Riggio, he listed the ques-

FIGURE 3-2   How our brain loses things along the way.

tions he would ask if he were in Riggio's shoes, along with the answers Duffy would give in response. According to Hay, "When the time for the interview came, Duffy presented his answers and waited. Riggio reached for a drawer and pulled out a list of questions he had prepared. When he glanced through them he realized that they had all been answered. The two of them went to lunch to celebrate the deal."

To be a great asker yourself, learn to ask "*W/H* questions," not yes/no questions: ask questions that begin with *Who, What, Where, When, Why,* and *How.* Yes/no questions close off further exploration of your topic; *W/H* questions open up possibilities for exploring your topic further.

One great tool for asking questions is the *reporter's checklist,* the set of six *W/H* questions listed in the preceding paragraph. Generations of reporters have learned these questions as a tool for getting the information they need from a source. I learned them from my father, the award-winning editor and publisher of a newspaper in rural Iowa. Whether writing about a town council meeting, a high school basketball game, or a wedding, I needed to be sure to get the *who, what, where, when, why,* and *how* of the event. Business writing is no different. Whenever human beings do something, there are always six *W/H* questions that can be asked and answered. If you ask and answer these questions here at the planning stage, before you begin drafting, you'll be able to draft with less interruption and more continuity, and you'll have to make fewer trips back to the store to buy nails.

(Incidentally, the reporter's checklist also can be useful at the revising stage as a check to make sure that you've included essential information. If you're like me, perhaps a fourth or a third of the meeting announcements and invitations I receive on the job omit the answer to one of the six *W/H* questions and therefore require a follow-up message or phone call.)

Another good list of questions is shown in Figure 3-3. It's the *four pairs.* Together, these eight questions can give you eight ways of looking at any subject, ways you otherwise may not have considered. Suppose that you've been asked to research and write a report on a possible supplier. As you look at the first box, "Same," you ask yourself, "How is this supplier like others with whom we've done—or might do—business?" As you look at the next box, "Different," you might ask, "What sets this supplier apart? What is it doing differently from others in this business?"

The next box, "Whole," invites you to think of the supplier's industry: "What are the common elements that run across this business area?" The box headed "Parts" encourages you to ask such questions as, "What is the internal structure of this supplier? Who are the key players?"

As you move to the box headed "Time," you begin to think historically: "How did this company get started? How long has it been around? What have

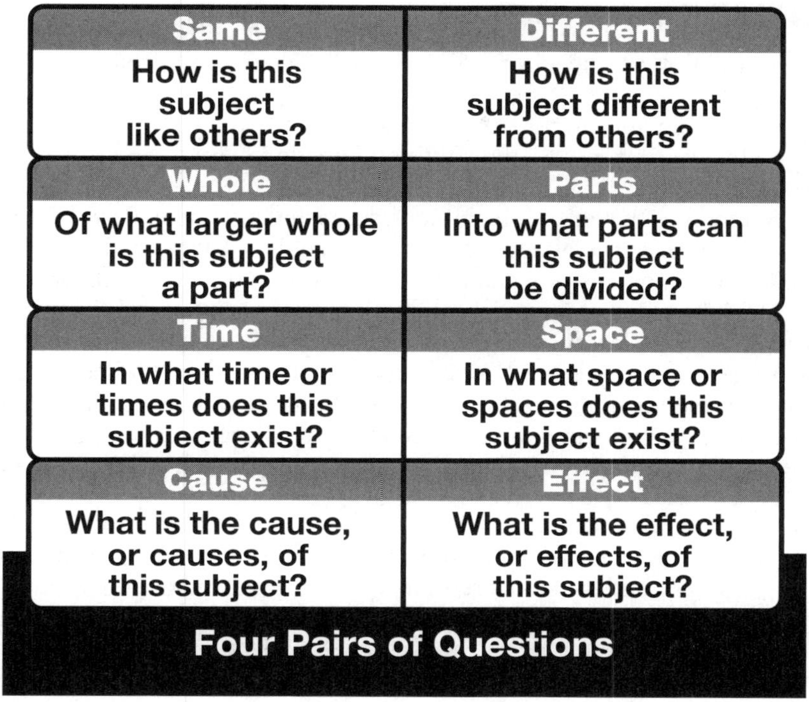

Same	Different
How is this subject like others?	How is this subject different from others?
Whole	**Parts**
Of what larger whole is this subject a part?	Into what parts can this subject be divided?
Time	**Space**
In what time or times does this subject exist?	In what space or spaces does this subject exist?
Cause	**Effect**
What is the cause, or causes, of this subject?	What is the effect, or effects, of this subject?

Four Pairs of Questions

FIGURE 3-3   Four pairs of questions.

been its ups and downs?" But you also consider time's other direction: "What is the future of this supplier?" The box headed "Space" suggests questions of location and context: "Where did this supplier get started? What's the reach of its market?"

The "Cause" box may lead to such questions as "Why are we considering this supplier? What led us to consider this company?" The box labeled "Effect" might suggest such questions as "What can go wrong if we enter into a relationship with this supplier? What can go right?"

As I hope you can see, the value of these questions lies in their appropriateness to any subject and in the wealth of further questions they can lead you to. However, don't worry if you can't always get results from all eight boxes; sometimes the chart will be useful in helping you to come up with just one new angle on your subject. In short, think of the eight questions as prods for brainstorming, and use them to guide you as you jot down all the questions or ideas you can think of.

OUTSIDE AND INSIDE

The information you need for a piece of writing can come from two places:

- Outside your mind—the stuff you don't know yet
- Inside your mind—the stuff you already know

Sometimes the best source of materials is other people. Particularly for very new or very specialized information, people working in the field will be able to give you answers you can't find in books or periodicals or online.

Don't be afraid to approach people, even very busy or well-known people, with requests for information. E-mail has made such requests relatively easy to answer. However, also consider phone or face-to-face requests. Because of the possibility of follow-up questions, as well as the nuances that can be conveyed by facial expression and tone of voice, even a very short face-to-face or phone interview can be extremely valuable. When you conduct an interview, consider this advice:

1. *Prepare in advance.* Read what you can find by or about the interviewee, and make a preliminary list of questions you would like answered.
2. *Break the ice.* Take a few seconds to establish a context for the interview and a relationship with the interviewee.
3. *Ask basic W/H questions.* Avoid multiple-choice and yes/no questions.
4. *Listen.* Don't be so worried about what your next question will be that you fail to hear the answer to the one you've just asked.
5. *Ask follow-up questions.* When points in an answer intrigue or confuse you or suggest whole new lines of inquiry to you, follow up on those points immediately. Don't continue down your list of prepared questions until you've fully explored the answer to each question you've already posed.
6. *Write down what you've learned as soon as possible.* Notes, even recordings, get "cold"; translate them into readable language while they're still warm.

For information from written sources, learn to be a good user of libraries and online resources. The Web has, of course, revolutionized research, and search engines such as Google are getting better by the month. However, the Web is the least reliable of sources: It contains both the best and most accurate and the worst and least accurate information. Therefore, use it critically, always asking yourself about the person or organization behind the page you're reading.

Besides turning to your computer for information, also build an efficient personal library. Keep close to your desk the books and files that you find yourself consulting often. These might include a dictionary, an atlas, and the specialized reference books of your business or profession. Also post prominently at your desk the phone number and Uniform Resource Locator (URL) of the reference department of your local public or university library. Reference librarians can supply a great amount of information for free, over the phone or online.

For "inside" information—the stuff you already know—this step in the planning stage gives you the opportunity to remind yourself of the information you already have and to pull it together into notes or a list. Consider doing some brainstorming in writing: jot down ideas as quickly as you can, without being concerned about the order they're in or even whether or not you'll use them eventually. At the next step, "Get Your Ducks in a Row" (Chapter 4), you'll have a chance to organize and filter this information.

MAP YOUR INFORMATION

My own favorite information-gathering tool—a tool I use often at this step of my writing process—is *mind-mapping*. This tool has been popularized widely by Englishman Tony Buzan and American Michael Gelb.

To mind-map, write your main topic or purpose in the center of a large sheet of paper. Perhaps even draw a picture to illustrate it and to engage nonverbal areas of your brain. Then begin drawing branches out from it as subtopics or associations come to mind. Consider doing more drawings, as well as making your map multicolored. In a very short time—well within the five minutes we've allotted to this step in the typical writing hour—you can produce a striking visual aid to use as you continue writing.

Training magazine has reported that the DFS Group, a retailer of luxury goods, has reduced meeting times 40 to 60 percent and trimmed 35 percent off information technology costs by using mind-mapping, supported by the software package MindManager.

Figure 3-4 is a copy of the map I drew using Mindmapper, another excellent piece of software, before I began drafting this chapter. If you compare this map with the resulting chapter, you'll see that I ended up organizing my material somewhat differently than I did on the map. But the map certainly served its purpose, helping me survey my topic and make preliminary decisions about what I wanted to include.

Editor and publisher Thomas McCormack has said, "Directors, coaches, and editors cannot teach you how to get there. But they can put you on the paths that lead there." Think of the techniques of this chapter—mind-mapping, brainstorming, the reporter's checklist, interviewing, and others—as paths you can take to find the information you need. Whatever paths you take, however, get your stuff together before you start drafting. Then your one-hour assembly job can be done in an hour, with much more effective results.

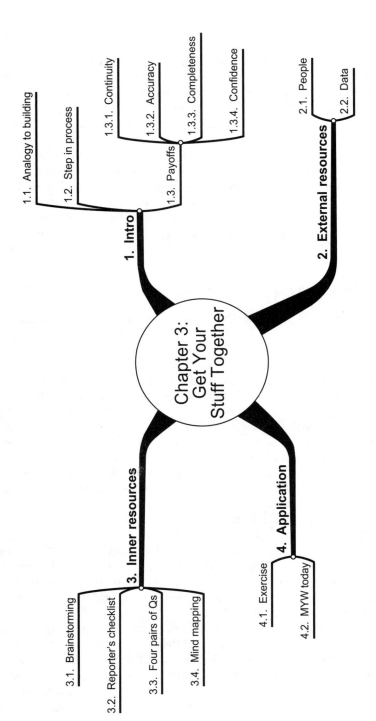

FIGURE 3-4 Mind map for Chapter 3.

EXERCISE

The following questions will test your understanding of this chapter. The final examination for this course will include similar questions.

1. Why is gathering information the third step in the planning stage?

    a. It should be done after defining your community—writer and reader(s)—and after defining your purpose.

    b. It should be done before organizing the content of your message.

    c. Both *a* and *b* are true.

    d. Neither *a* nor *b* is true.

2. Why should gathering information be done before drafting?

    a. To reduce interruptions during drafting

    b. To reduce the possibility of leaving out important information

    c. To give you the confidence to draft more easily

    d. All of the above

3. What kinds of questions are usually best to ask in an interview?

    a. Yes/no questions

    b. Multiple-choice questions

    c. Who, what, where, when, why, and how questions

    d. None of the above

4. The reporter's checklist can be valuable at what stage(s) of the writing process?

    a. The planning stage

    b. The revising stage

    c. Both *a* and *b*

    d. Neither *a* nor *b*

5. The four pairs of questions for gathering information are based on which of the following sets of words?

    a. Personality, attitude(s), circumstances, knowledge

    b. Same/different, whole/parts, time/space, cause/effect

    c. *Ko* and *mei*

    d. None of the above

6. Which of the following is *not* good advice for interviewing?

   a. Prepare for the interview by reading and by listing questions.

   b. Don't be distracted from your list of questions by the interviewee's responses.

   c. Ask basic *W/H* questions.

   d. Write down what you've learned as soon as possible.

7. Which of these statements about information on the Web is most true?

   a. Web-based information is almost always accurate.

   b. Web-based information is almost always inaccurate.

   c. Web-based information can be accurate or inaccurate, so it should be read and used critically.

   d. Web-based information can be accurate or inaccurate, so it should not be used.

8 Which of the following is *not* good advice for brainstorming in writing?

   a. Jot down ideas as quickly as you can.

   b. Don't be concerned about the order ideas are in.

   c. List only those ideas that you're sure you'll use in the piece of writing.

   d. Answers *a, b,* and *c* are all good advice.

9. Which of the following statements about mind-mapping is true?

   a. A mind map should include only the information you'll use in the piece of writing.

   b. A mind map should map information in the order in which it will be used in the piece of writing.

   c. An effective mind map can be done only by computer.

   d. None of these statements is true.

10. Any writing you do at the information-gathering stage should have which of the following characteristics?

   a. It should be carefully spelled and punctuated.

   b. It should be based on your definitions of audience and purpose for the writing job.

   c. It should be carefully organized.

   d. All of the above.

MANAGE YOUR WRITING *TODAY*

Now that you've checked your understanding of Chapter 3, you should put it into practice right away.

- On the very next writing job you have to do, begin with some writing management: Remind yourself that you're a writer, that writing can be managed, and that it's largely a matter of managing time. Set up blocks of time for planning, drafting, and revising—with more time allocated for planning and revising than for drafting.

- Then begin the planning stage by "finding the 'we.'" Take perhaps five minutes to ask yourself, "What is the smallest community to which my audience and I both belong?" and "How are my audience and I alike and different in the four PACK dimensions: personality, attitude, circumstances, and knowledge?" Then take another five minutes to "make holes, not drills" by defining the purpose of the piece of writing. Ask yourself, "Is my purpose to tell my reader(s) about something, ask my reader(s) to do something, or both? Will this piece of writing function as conversation, correspondence, covenant, or conception—or some combination of those?"

- Then practice what you've learned in this chapter, taking as long as you need, at first, to gather information for the piece of writing. Use the reporter's checklist, my four pairs, or both. Go to resources, human and written, for the external information you need, and do brainstorming or mind-mapping for the information you already have in your head.

- Now go ahead and do the rest of your planning, thinking about structure. (You'll learn specific organizing methods in the next chapter.)

- Then draft your document with as little editing as possible.

- Take a break.

- Then revise it.

When you've finished the writing job, take a few minutes to evaluate how the process worked for you. Evaluate especially whether "getting your stuff together" in advance resulted in a more effective message at the end.

C H A P T E R

GET YOUR DUCKS IN A ROW
MANAGE YOUR STRUCTURE

N THE FIRST SEASON of the TV series *M*A*S*H*, the compound comes under heavy bombardment, but one bomb doesn't explode. Instead, it has nosed its way into the ground in the center of the compound and just sits there ticking. If it's not defused soon, it will blow up. Frank Burns faints, so Hawkeye Pierce and Trapper John McIntyre are left to defuse the bomb. Colonel Henry Blake secures a copy of the defusing instructions, which he reads aloud to Hawkeye and Trapper from behind a sandbag bunker.

"First you need a wrench," he shouts. Hawkeye and Trapper find one. "Place it gently on the nut just above the locking ring and loosen," he continues. They do so. "Now rotate the locking ring counterclockwise." They do.

"Now remove the tail assembly," he reads, "and carefully cut the wires leading to the clockwork fuse at the head." Out come the wire cutters. Snip, snip. . . .

". . . but first, remove the fuse."

The resulting explosion dramatizes what is perhaps the chief difficulty of putting things in writing: writing is linear. As shown in Figure 4-1, it is made up of one word, phrase, or sentence after another. It is read most often in a "straight line" from beginning to end. Writing is like tape storage for a computer, requiring movement along the line of tape in order to record or access information.

Thought, on the other hand, is usually not linear. When we know something, we know it "all at once" as a network of simultaneous, interconnected ideas, as shown in Figure 4-2. Thought is like random-access memory (RAM), with any information available at any time.

FIGURE 4-1   Writing is linear.

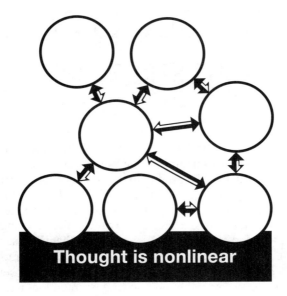

FIGURE 4-2   Thought is nonlinear.

Changing nonlinear thought into linear language is one of the most difficult steps in the writing process. Therefore, this chapter is one of the most important in this book. At this point in the planning stage,

- We have "found the 'we'" by defining our readers and the relationship we have with them.
- We have "made holes, not drills" by defining our purpose in writing.
- We have "got our stuff together" by gathering the information we need for the job.

Now we end the planning stage, as shown in Figure 4-3, by "getting our ducks in a row," organizing this particular information to achieve this particular purpose for this particular reader.

FIGURE 4-3   Get your ducks in a row.

The writer of the bomb-defusing instructions knew his subject as a total set of interrelated actions, but he forgot that readers can read only one word, phrase, or sentence at a time. The result was—to say the least—a less than effective piece of writing. To be effective, a piece of writing must be organized. It must present its information in the order that best serves the writer's purpose and the reader's needs.

Lee Wood, a writer at Resort Condominiums International, says that she loves reading documents in which "the writer was so kind as to put himself in my shoes and give me the information in the order I can use it." Most readers are like Lee. A little extra work for the writer will save a lot of extra work for the reader—and increase the reader's goodwill.

AN EVERYDAY EXAMPLE

Fortunately, most of us don't have to write life-and-death instructions every day (as mentioned in Chapter 1 when I was talking about the fighter-plane ejection instructions). However, attention to organization can help even our most routine messages. Consider this memo, which I was given by a client at a Fortune 100 company:

SUBJECT: Roadway identification in parking lots

During our Safety Coordinators' meeting the point was made that with our energy conservation program (during the hours of darkness, fog, etc.) roadway identification in our parking lots is hazardous. The recommendation was raised that we might use a fluorescent-type reflecting paint. Would you please investigate the feasibility of this recommendation and advise me as to your decision on implementation?

Your early response is appreciated.

Don't get me wrong. This is not terrible writing. The memo is short enough that it probably will get the job done no matter how it's written. But if you're like most readers I've shown this memo to, you found it difficult to follow. You even may have had to read it twice or three times to understand what it meant. Or you may have given up without understanding.

I'm pretty sure that the writer of this memo was a one-stage writer, as described in the introduction. I can see her coming from the safety coordinators' meeting, sitting down with a keyboard or pad of paper, and writing this memo a sentence at a time—planning, drafting, and revising each sentence before moving on to the next one. And like the writer from M*A*S*H, she seems to have put the information down in the order in which she thought of it, not in the order in which the reader can use it.

The first thing the writer apparently thought of was the meeting she had just left, so she began with that. Then she thought of the problem that was raised at the meeting, the problem she was writing about, so she continued her sentence with that. In the middle of this first sentence she seems to have had a flicker of realization that the relationship between energy conservation and roadway identification might not be clear to her reader, so she interrupted the sentence for a parenthetical explanation. She then thought of the solution that was suggested for the problem, so she wrote a sentence about that. She then thought of what she wanted the reader to do, so she made that her third sentence. Finally, she thought about needing an answer soon, so she made that the last sentence of the memo. Like Allen in Figure 4-4, she simply captured ideas as they came to her. And from her point of view—the writer's point of view—that organization made perfect sense.

From the reader's point of view—your point of view in this case—the sense of the memo was probably less than perfect. The first sentence starts with a meeting the reader did not attend and may not have even known about. So already the reader is asking, consciously or subconsciously, WIIFM?—What's In It For Me? After the mention of the meeting, the reader encounters the energy conservation program and then a phrase that looks like an explanation (it's in parentheses, after all), but it doesn't explain anything that's been said so far. Moreover, the parenthetical phrase interrupts the flow of the first sentence, so by the time the reader gets to the end of that sentence, he prob-

FIGURE 4-4   New ideas rush into Allen's mind pell-mell, crowding old ones out before they take form or shape.

ably has to go back and reread it in order to make sense of it. And even if he does work out what that sentence means, he's still asking WIIFM?

If the memo were from anybody other than the reader's boss, he might not continue reading. Since it's from his boss, though, he goes on. The second sentence seems to be a response to the point raised in the first sentence, but even so, the WIIFM problem remains. Finally, in the third sentence, the WIIFM question gets answered, in the form of an assignment. The reader's attention perks up at that, so he probably goes back to the beginning again to try to understand what he is being asked to do. In all, from the reader's point of view, reading this short memo has been much more difficult—and annoying—than necessary.

This is why this step in the writing process is so important. As Frank Smith, a leading researcher into the reading process, has written, "An enormous advantage of writing over speech is that ideas can easily be reorganized in both time and space. They do not have to remain in the order in which they are produced." Here's my suggested revision to the parking lot memo. I don't claim that it's Pulitzer Prize–winning prose, only that it presents information in an order that the reader can use it—an order more likely to get the results the writer wants:

SUBJECT: Fluorescent paint in parking lots

Can we use fluorescent paint in our parking lots to make traffic lanes easier to see?

During our Safety Coordinators' meeting, someone pointed out that with our reduced lighting, roadways are hard to see in fog or darkness.

Please find out whether this solution will work, and let me know within a week.

Thanks.

As you see, this memo begins with what the writer wants the reader to do. And because what the reader is being asked to do is answer a question, the sentence is worded as a question. After reading the first sentence, the reader knows immediately what he's being asked to do: give a yes-or-no answer to a specific query. Then, and only then, is he given the background information that will help him to move toward an answer.

Sports agent Mark H. McCormack has written that "a lot of memos would be more persuasive if their first and last paragraphs were switched."

THE TECHNIQUE OF ORGANIZING

It is sometimes possible to reorganize a piece of writing, as McCormack implies, at the revising stage of the process. After all, that's when I reorganized the parking lot memo. But that's a little like changing the floor plan of a house after you've built it. Yes, you could conceivably cut the garage off a completed house and move it to the other end of the building, but that's certainly not the best time to do it. Organizing your information, like laying out the rooms of a house, is best done at the planning stage. As the great twentieth-century philosopher Winnie the Pooh said, "Organizing is what you do before you do something, so that when you do it, it's not all mixed up."

I deliberately have not yet used the dreaded *O* word because I fear that for many readers the word *outline* will call up junior-high memories of Roman numerals, capital letters, Arabic numerals, and lower-case letters all in exactly the right order and spaced and punctuated just right. If you're like me, when you had to turn in a formal outline with your finished paper, you wrote the paper first and then made an outline that matched it. Of course, if you find formal outlines useful for organizing information, by all means use them. But formal outlines certainly aren't necessary at this step in the writing process. For example, when executive Donald Walton talks about the importance of outlining, he clearly means something pretty informal: "Even if I'm writing something as brief as a one-page letter," he says, "I like to jot down some sort of outline. It may consist of no more than three or four words or phrases: the essence of thought I want to get across and the order in which I intend to build my message."

Walton is right. A good plan at this point in the process may consist of only three or four words or phrases. If you've already jotted down some words or phrases in step 3, then step 4 may consist only of numbering those words or phrases: "Let's see, I'll put this in paragraph 2, this in paragraph 4, this I'll leave out, this in paragraph 1, this also in paragraph 2, this in paragraph 3, and this and this I'll also leave out." If you've made a mind map, you can simply number its branches in the best order for your reader. (In MindManager, you can drag branches around on your screen and then, if you wish, ask the program to number them in clockwise order.)

As you see, for most short letters and memos, you may need only a minute or two to decide what information your reader should get first, second, and third. By taking that minute or two to "get your ducks in a row," you'll be doing your reader a great service. You'll also be making the writing process easier for yourself. When you have decided in advance what the main sections of your piece of writing will be and in what order they will come, you won't have to interrupt your drafting to make those decisions. And because you have divided your writing task into parts, you will have turned a long, complicated writing job into several shorter, simpler ones. You then can write your letter, memo, or speech one paragraph or section at a time.

For example, as I'm drafting this, next to my computer table is another table with a separate pile of notes for each of the sections I've planned for this chapter. I gathered those notes in step 3 and arranged them into piles in step 4. Now as I draft, in step 5, all I have to do is go through the piles in order, drafting a section at a time.

FORMULAS

Most writing handbooks devote a lot of space to formulas—prewritten outlines—for organizing various kinds of business writing: job application letters, collection letters, and the like. And don't worry; this book will give you some too. However, it is important to remember that in any given business situation, you know more than the textbook author. You have defined

- the audience,
- the purpose,
- and the information content

for the particular writing job you have to do, so give yourself credit. After all the careful work you've done in steps 1, 2, and 3, don't just fall back on some textbook formula in step 4. Whether or not you find a formula to base your writing on, you'll be most effective if you ask yourself, "What order should I put this particular information in, for this purpose, for this reader?"

Still, formulas can be helpful as a starting place. Here are four that I find especially useful:

1. Requests for Information

One of the easiest kinds of business communication is a request for information; usually no psychological complications come between writer and reader. Careless organization, however, can make information harder to get. The parking lot memo earlier in this chapter is an example.

When you write a request for information, consider following the plan shown in Figure 4-5. Note that your first paragraph specifically asks for the information you want. If you can put this request in question form, all the better; you will signal more clearly to the reader that he or she is expected to answer your request.

Then—and this is important—put in a paragraph break. One important purpose of paragraphing is to signal the major divisions of a piece of writing. A paragraph break after this first question will help to emphasize it.

In your next paragraph or paragraphs, provide any additional information the reader may need. You may not need this paragraph, nor may your reader; this is why it is boxed with dotted lines in the diagram. If your question has several parts, summarize it in the first paragraph, and then, after giving background, break it into a numbered list of specific questions. This numbering will make it easy for your reader to answer your questions without repeating them. He or she can just write, for example,

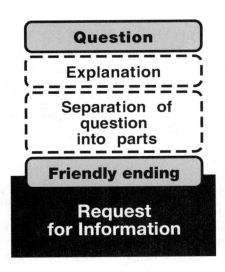

FIGURE 4-5   Request for information.

1. Yes.
2. $13,000.
3. Only if we receive the order by January 1.

The ending of your request will be the last thing your reader reads, so you'll want it to leave a good impression. Avoid flowery, "rubber stamp" endings like "Thank you in advance" or "Begging to remain yours truly." Such endings only sound stilted and insincere. If you know your reader well enough to close with a personal reference, by all means, do so ("Thanks for your help with the Oswald report, Carmen; I'm glad we're working together again on this one."). Otherwise, a simple "Thanks" or "Thank you" is usually better than a longer, more formal close.

2. Claims

Claims—requests for the remedy of a problem—require a somewhat different strategy. Making the request in the first sentence may be too abrupt and threatening and so may increase resistance to solving your problem. A letter that begins "Please repair or replace our Ace-High Water Cooler immediately" may generate an unnecessarily negative response.

Instead of putting your request first, try putting the problem first, inviting your reader to become an ally instead of an enemy. (When you "found the 'we'" in step 1, you defined a basis for this alliance.) Be clear and forceful, of course, but also give your reader a way to solve your problem while still "saving face." For example, you might write the letter this way:

Our Ace-High Water Cooler has been giving our water a yellowish color and plastic taste.

We bought the cooler last month under a one-year warranty. The unpleasant color and taste of the water began the first week. We emptied the cooler and washed and rinsed the water bottle thoroughly, but the color and taste have continued.

Will you please repair or replace the cooler as soon as possible? Or if you wish, simply refund its cost.

Thank you.

Try the formula shown in Figure 4-6. In your first paragraph, state the problem and nothing else; this will give your reader the necessary context for the rest of your message. Next, provide background, if necessary. Only then offer a clear solution. When possible, give your reader a choice of acceptable solutions; such a choice will keep your reader from feeling cornered and will increase the chances of compliance. As always, try for a friendly ending.

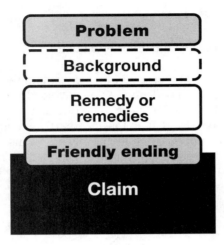

FIGURE 4-6   Claim.

3. Good-News Responses

Giving your reader good news is like rowing downstream: you have everything going for you. Therefore, as shown in Figure 4-7, begin with the good news so that your reader will recognize it immediately and be pleased by it. Begin, perhaps, with the word *yes*. The word *you* is a good second choice. Then insert a paragraph break as a way of emphasizing the good news.

The following paragraph(s), if necessary, should carry any qualifications or additional information. The qualifications should never constitute a retreat from the good news: "Yes, you will receive the raise you requested at such time as it can be accurately determined that hell has frozen over."

The closing paragraph should be a friendly ending, but remember, not a rubber-stamp one.

4. Bad-News Responses

When you have to give bad news, you naturally have a much harder job. You are rowing upstream, against the current of the reader's attitudes. Therefore, consider beginning, as shown in Figure 4-8, with a neutral statement establishing the context for the response.

Then move to the reasons or process that led to the negative decision. Finally, state the bad news, but follow it immediately with a goodwill message. If this message can offer the reader something as a compromise, all the better.

When you have bad news to give, nothing you can do as a writer will guarantee the reader's goodwill. However, by organizing your message care-

FIGURE 4-7   Good-news response.

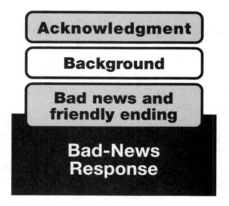

FIGURE 4-8   Bad-news response.

fully, you can at least increase the probability that your reader will read and understand the reasons for the bad news.

HOW TO CHANGE MINDS

When I asked more than a hundred business leaders, "What are your three biggest communication problems?" the number two answer (after "speaking to a group") was "being persuasive." These leaders recognized that the essence of leadership is having a vision, communicating it to others, and influencing them to follow. Effective communicators need to know how to change minds.

When your purpose is to persuade your reader, you can use either of two basic strategies—direct or indirect. Direct persuasion dates from ancient Greece and is based on the assumption that your reader is a reasonable person who will be persuaded by good reasons. In direct persuasion, you simply state your position and then list reasons for it.

If you have written school papers that were based on a *thesis statement,* then you have used direct persuasion in writing. A thesis statement is simply a statement of a position, which is then supported by reasons in the rest of a paper. The following first paragraph of a letter to a U.S. senator ends with a traditional thesis statement, which the rest of the letter goes on to support.

> As you know, the U.S. government has been purchasing dairy cattle from farmers since the middle of 1986. In my opinion, the whole-herd dairy buy-out program, as it is called, was a mistake.

Indirect persuasion is also ancient in its use but has not been taught formally until recently. It is based on the assumption that your reader may have an opposing position that she may not easily give up. Efforts to confront such a reader directly may lead not to successful persuasion but to a hardening of the reader's original position. Therefore, indirect persuasion attempts to gain the reader's acceptance by creating an atmosphere of cooperation and mutual understanding.

Abraham Lincoln was talking about indirect persuasion when he said, "If you would win a man to your cause, first convince him that you are his sincere friend."

To persuade indirectly, begin by stating the problem objectively and, especially, by stating the opposing position accurately. By doing so, you demonstrate that you are a fair person who can see things through your opponents' eyes. Having done this, you can even go a step further, stating the circumstances in which your opponents' position is, in fact, the right one.

At this point your relationship with your reader should be firmly established, so you can proceed safely to state your position and the circumstances in which it is the correct one.

Notice that you have not threatened or alienated your reader by opposing her position. Instead, you have agreed with it, at least in certain circumstances. All you have done is shown that circumstances also exist in which *your* position is right.

With this balance established between the two positions, you can then go ahead to tip the balance your way, by showing that the circumstances in which your position is the right one are the circumstances that exist now. Better still, sometimes you can present your position as simply a desirable modification of the opposing one, or you can suggest a combination of both positions as the best solution.

Here's an example of indirect persuasion:

Thank you for asking me to comment on Dwight's proposal that Casey and Evans begin direct mail-order sales of our product line. The proposal obviously has been thought out carefully; it includes impressive statistics on the profit potential of mail-order sales and a detailed plan for building a mailing list and handling the shipment of orders.

The proposal is a sound one. In these days of two-income families and busy schedules, consumers are finding it increasingly convenient to shop by mail. Moreover, the mail-order companies that have earned high brand-name recognition are enjoying the benefits of direct marketing.

However, new companies just entering the mail-order industry—companies without existing recognition and reputation—are not doing well. Given the state of the economy and the high prices for printing and postage, this is not a good time for such companies to begin mail-order sales.

Unfortunately, Casey and Evans is such a company; while we have a reputation among retailers for quality novelty items, that recognition does not extend to the consumer. I suggest, therefore, that Dwight's excellent proposal be postponed until economic conditions improve. Meanwhile, Casey and Evans should begin to give our brand name greater prominence on our products. I believe that in the future we might well want to move into mail-order sales.

Whichever strategy you adopt, keep in mind the basic principles of persuasion. Psychologist Robert B. Cialdina, after 30 years of research into what makes people comply with requests, identified six human tendencies that can lead to compliance:

1. *Reciprocation.* People more likely will give you something if they get something back.
2. *Consistency.* If people comply with one request, they more likely will comply with others.
3. *Social validation.* People more likely will comply if others are complying.
4. *Liking.* People more likely will comply with requests from people they like.
5. *Authority.* People more likely will comply with requests from people they see as being in authority.
6. *Scarcity.* People more likely will comply with requests when they see what they will receive as scarce.

FROM INFORMATION TO KNOWLEDGE

Remember that the first sentence of the introduction to this book referred to the *knowledge economy.* I prefer that term to the terms *information age* and *information economy* because information by itself has no value. To be valuable, information must be organized and communicated and thus turned into knowledge.

Futurist John Naisbitt, in his visionary book, *Megatrends*, wrote, "We are drowning in information but starved for knowledge." Software entrepreneur Neil Larson offered the solution: "Knowledge is information with structure." And knowledge management guru Thomas A. Stewart wrote, "Intelligence becomes an asset when some useful order is created out of free-floating brainpower."

So when you spend five minutes or so on step 4, "getting your ducks in a row," you are doing much more than a writing exercise. You are converting information into knowledge, intelligence into an asset. You are helping solve a piece of your reader's information-overload problem. You are truly creating value in a knowledge economy.

EXERCISES

Exercise A

The following questions will test your understanding of this chapter. The final examination for this course will include similar questions.

1. Why is organizing information the fourth step in the planning stage?

   a. It should be done after defining your community, defining your purpose, and gathering your information.

   b. It should be done before drafting your message.

   c. Both *a* and *b* are true.

   d. Neither *a* nor *b* is true.

2. Why should organizing be done before drafting?

   a. To reduce interruptions during drafting

   b. To allow you to focus on the best order for the reader

   c. To turn the drafting job into a series of smaller jobs

   d. All the above

3. Which of the following is a common difficulty with writing?

   a. It requires converting linear thinking into nonlinear writing.

   b. It requires converting nonlinear thinking into linear writing.

   c. It requires converting static thinking into active writing.

   d. None of the above.

4. Which of the following is(are) characteristic(s) of one-stage writers?

   a. They write in the order they think of things.

   b. They write in the most effective order for the reader.

   c. Both *a* and *b*

   d. Neither *a* nor *b*

5. Should formal outlines be used at the planning stage?

   a. Yes, they should always be used.

   b. No, they should never be used.

   c. They should be used only if they are useful to the writer.

   d. They should be used only when writing speeches.

6. Unless you have a good reason otherwise, how should routine requests for information begin?

   a. With background information

   b. With the request itself, phrased as a question if possible

   c. With friendly, personal information

   d. With the reason for the request

7. Unless you have a good reason otherwise, how should claims begin?

   a. With background information

   b. With the request itself, phrased as a question if possible

   c. With friendly, personal information

   d. With a statement of the problem

8. Unless you have a good reason otherwise, how should good-news responses begin?

   a. With background information

   b. With the good news

   c. With friendly, personal information

   d. With any qualifications about the good news

9. Unless you have a good reason otherwise, how should bad-news responses begin?

   a. With background information

   b. With the bad news

   c. With an acknowledgment of the request

   d. With any qualifications about the bad news

10. Which of the following is *not* a feature of indirect persuasion?

   a. It begins with a clear statement of your position.

   b. It begins with a clear statement of the problem.

   c. It acknowledges and clearly states your opponents' position(s).

   d. It describes the circumstances in which your opponents' position is correct.

Exercise B

You are a tax accountant. One of your clients is Dr. Barbara Smith, a retired university professor. Recently, she received a letter from the Internal Revenue Service (IRS) proposing that her latest tax return was incorrect.

   You are writing a response to the IRS and have listed the following facts. Number the facts in the order you would include them in your letter.

   a. The IRS claims that three payments to Dr. Smith were not listed as income on her tax return.

   b. The letter from the IRS was headed "Proposed Changes to Income" and was dated December 2, 20XX.

   c. Of the Teachers Insurance and Annuity Association payment of $1,213, $516 was reported on Schedule B as dividends.

   d. The College Retirement Equity annuity of $2,656 indeed appears to have been omitted from the return.

   e. Dr. Smith operates a business that includes writing.

   f. Of the Teachers Insurance and Annuity Association payment, $697 was reported on line 16 as fully taxable pension.

   g. You want the IRS to send Dr. Smith a revised tax bill.

   h. Dr. Smith's Social Security Number is XXX-XX-XXXX.

   i. The book royalties of $275 were included in the $4,660 gross receipts on Schedule C as business income.

MANAGE YOUR WRITING *TODAY*

Now that you've checked your understanding of Chapter 4, you should put it into practice right away.

   ■ On the very next writing job you have to do, begin with some writing management: Remind yourself that you're a writer, that writing can be managed, and that it's largely a matter of managing time. Set up blocks of time for planning, drafting, and revising—with more time allocated for planning and revising than for drafting.

- Then begin the planning stage by "finding the 'we.'" Take perhaps five minutes to ask yourself, "What is the smallest community to which my audience and I both belong?" and "How are my audience and I alike and different in the four PACK dimensions: personality, attitude, circumstances, and knowledge?" Then take another five minutes to "make holes, not drills" by defining the purpose of the piece of writing. Ask yourself, "Is my purpose to tell my reader(s) about something, ask my reader(s) to do something, or both? Will this piece of writing function as conversation, correspondence, covenant, or conception—or some combination of those?" Take another five minutes or so to gather information for the piece of writing. Use the reporter's checklist, my four pairs, or both. Go to resources, human and written, for the external information you need, and do brainstorming or mind-mapping for the information you already have in your head.

- Now spend as much time as you need on organizing this information to best achieve your purpose for your reader(s). If your writing task is a request for information, claim, or good-news or bad-news response, begin with one of the formulas in this chapter. If your task is persuasion, decide whether to use direct or indirect persuasion. Make whatever kind of outline or numbered list that seems to work for you.

- Then draft your document with as little editing as possible.

- Take a break.

- Then revise it.

When you've finished the writing job, take a few minutes to evaluate how the process worked for you. Evaluate especially whether "getting your ducks in a row" in advance resulted in a more effective piece of writing at the end.

5

DO IT WRONG THE FIRST TIME

MANAGE YOUR DRAFTING

WE'VE FINISHED the planning stage of the writing process, so we're ready to draft. We've defined our reader(s), defined our purpose, gathered our information, and decided how to organize that information. Now, at the drafting stage, it's time to actually write the document for the first time.

As you've seen, this step is "Do It Wrong the First Time." In this age of zero defects, total quality management, Six Sigma, and ISO-whatever, this advice may seem like heresy. However, as Ken Blanchard and Robert Lorber wrote in *Putting the One Minute Manager to Work,* "Anything worth doing does not have to be done perfectly—at first." Remember that, as Figure 5-1 shows, we're only about 25 minutes into the typical writing hour. We can afford to make mistakes now in the interest of a better result at the end. We'll have time later to make the document perfect.

Great novelists have always known the truth of doing it wrong the first time. William Faulkner advised, "Get it down. Take chances. It may be bad, but it's the only way you can do anything really good." And Bernard DeVoto wrote, "The best reason for putting anything down on

FIGURE 5-1   Do it wrong the first time.

paper is that one may then change it." We business writers can learn from them.

DRAFT AS PROTOTYPE

I learned the reason for doing it wrong the first time not from novelists but from a group of managers I was training at a manufacturing site of a Fortune 100 company. Our training room was lined with motivational posters proclaiming such principles as "Think," "Quality Comes First," and yes, "Do It Right the First Time." My group of managers quickly challenged my directive to "Do It Wrong the First Time." I realized that these managers saw me as just a crazy consultant from outside who was clueless about their strong quality-oriented corporate culture.

For once, I knew what to do. The plant where I was working made printers, so I asked the managers to tell me the story of how their company developed and manufactured a new printer model.

Well, they said, we put together a planning team from a variety of specialties. There's a marketer who talks about what will sell next year. There's an engineer who lets the team know what new technologies are available. There's a money person who brings a budget framework for the project. And so on. Together they begin envisioning the new printer. As they work, more and more engineers are brought in to convert the team's vision into more and more detailed blueprints.

And then, the managers said, these high-priced designers turn the blueprints over to Charlie. And Charlie goes into his shop and actually builds the printer. Charlie has to form a sheet-metal case manually, of course. And because he may not have the integrated circuits yet, he may have to do some hard wiring. But before long, the first printer is made.

At this point in their story, I interrupted. "So Charlie makes sure to put the company's nameplate on that first printer?" I asked. "And he stamps it with serial number 1? Because you're eventually going to sell it, right?"

The managers laughed. "Of course not," they said. "The printer that Charlie builds is just a *prototype*. It's not built to sell; it's built just to test."

"Ah ha!" I gloated. "So you don't do it right the first time. Because you know you won't sell the prototype, it doesn't have to be perfect. Making it perfect—with the right nameplate and paint and all—would be a huge waste of time and would distract you from the more important features that have to be tested."

Now please understand that those flashes of insight are rare for me. But this time the managers helped me arrive at an insight that worked for them and that has worked for me ever since. When a company develops a new product, it doesn't worry about making the first one perfect, as if it will be sold to a customer. The first one or two—probably even the first one or two dozen—are prototypes, built for testing and refining. Building and testing these imperfect prototypes are important steps toward finally "doing it right."

This is not how most of us write, however. We try to skip the prototype stage and go right to the final product. Most of us edit carefully as we write, pausing every few words to check spelling or punctuation or grammar. But as novelist Robert Cormer has said, "The beautiful part of writing is that you don't have to get it right the first time, unlike, say, a brain surgeon."

A draft is a prototype. It is not the final product. It is not written for the reader. It is written for the writer. It is "quick and dirty." It is written to test. It is written to see if it does what it was planned to do.

When you move from the planning to the drafting stage, you do so because you can't plan the document any more. As author Natalie Goldberg has said, "Finally, one just has to shut up, sit down, and write." You just have to build a prototype to see if it works. In doing so, you're following the lead of management megaguru Tom Peters. "On the wall of my Vermont writing studio," he writes, "is a quote by David Kelley, founder of IDEO Product Design: 'Fail faster. Succeed sooner.' Next to it hangs a saying by the extraordinary photographer Diane Arbus, who told her students: 'Learn not to be careful.'"

EXERCISE

This chapter won't contribute any questions to the final examination. However, the exercise in this chapter is one of the most important in the course, so please do it.

- Find a 10-minute time period when you probably won't be interrupted. Turn off your cell phone. If you're at work and you have an office with a door, close it. Put up a sticky note that says, "Do not disturb." If you're at home, ask your family not to interrupt you for 10 minutes.

- Then, if you can type faster than you can write by hand, open a new document in your word-processing program. If you can write faster by hand, grab a smooth-writing pen and a couple of fresh sheets of paper.

- Notice the time, and then start writing. Write for 10 minutes as fast as you physically can, literally without stopping. Write "quick and dirty." Don't stop to think of what to say next. (If you have to, just write, "I don't know what to write. I don't know what to write. . . ." until you think of something to write.) Don't stop to read what you've written. Don't stop to correct spelling, punctuation, or grammar. Don't stop to change anything. (If you need to, turn off your computer monitor or turn its brightness all the way down.) In short, follow novelist John Steinbeck's advice: "Write freely and as rapidly as possible and throw the whole thing on paper. Never correct or rewrite until the whole thing is down."

- After 10 minutes, just stop.

DEBRIEFING THE EXERCISE

At the end of the 10 minutes, you may not have Pulitzer Prize–winning prose, but you will have achieved two things:

1. You've probably produced more writing than you've ever before generated in 10 minutes. According to language specialist Frank Smith, we can produce language, in the form of speech, at about 250 words a minute. A keyboard might slow us down to 50 words per minute. Even at the snail's pace of keyboarding or handwriting, however, the 5 minutes we've arbitrarily allocated for drafting should give us time to produce 250 words—all we need for a one-hour letter or memo. All of us can, in fact, write much faster than we normally do, as long as we don't plan or revise while we're drafting.

2. You've experienced what writing without editing can feel like. You may not have felt comfortable at first because there may have been a part of you that kept wanting to stop to fix things. (In the next chapter we'll talk about that part of you; we'll even give it a name.) However, perhaps by the end of the 10 minutes

you began to feel more comfortable. You may have experienced what writer Richard Andersen calls "get[ting] out of the words' way."

In a real situation, of course, you will have prepared for this quick and dirty draft by asking some important questions about your reader, purpose, subject matter, and organization. In short, you will have done the planning taught so far in this course. Even in a real situation, though, you can then draft virtually without stopping. If you don't know how to spell a word, you can just approximate; you or your spell-checker can fix it later. If you don't know which of two words to use, you can use them both; you can decide between them when you look at your draft again at the revising stage. For now, you just need to get comfortable with doing it wrong the first time. As the great editor Maxwell Perkins said, "Just get it down on paper, and then we'll see what to do with it."

You see, in the long run, stopping to edit while we draft breaks our train of thought and keeps us from being as smart or creative as we could be. Moreover, it commits us much too early to the illusion of perfection, keeping us from doing the later revision that could help our writing get its job done better. In the long run, getting it right the first time keeps us from communicating as effectively as we could. Our communication and our careers suffer.

Comedy writer Larry Gelbart has said it well: "You have to allow yourself the liberty of writing poorly. You have to get the bulk of it done, and then you start to refine it. You have to put down less than marvelous material just to keep going to whatever you think the end is going to be—which may be something else altogether by the time you get there."

OVERCOMING WRITER'S BLOCK

Journalist Gene Fowler once said, "Writing is easy; all you do is sit staring at a blank sheet of paper until the drops of blood form on your forehead." While most of us haven't literally had that experience, I suspect that most of us have suffered, like Cynthia in Figure 5-2, from writer's block.

In my experience—and in the experience of many writers with whom I've worked—writer's block is usually the result of fear. As James Waldroop, cofounder of the consulting firm Peregrine Partners, has written, "The enemy of a good decision is fear—fear of failure, fear of humiliation, fear of making a mistake."

The best way I know to get past that fear is to just start writing while giving yourself permission to do it wrong the first time. If it helps, send yourself an e-mail about why you can't get started writing. Before you know it, you're writing.

To overcome writer's block, follow Frank Smith's advice: "Do not expect the writing to come out right the first time. Do not be afraid of the possibility that what you write will fail to live up to your expectations, or those of the schoolteacher on your shoulder. Anything you write can be changed. Anything you write can be thrown away. You have nothing to lose."

FIGURE 5-2   Cynthia comes face to face with the possibility that brains may be self-cleaning.

WRITING AND "FLOW"

One way to understand the benefits of quick and dirty drafting—and of five-stage writing as a whole process—is based on the work of psychologist Mihaly Csikszentmihalyi (pronounced "chick sent me HIGH"). He observes that all human experiences provide varying degrees of challenge. For example, the experience of making toast for breakfast presents a fairly low level of challenge, whereas the experience of preparing a full Chinese banquet presents a higher level of challenge.

We meet life's challenges, says Csikszentmihalyi, with varying degrees of skill. A novice Chinese chef brings to the banquet preparation a relatively low level of skill; a veteran chef brings a much higher level.

Csikszentmihalyi writes that if the challenge presented by an experience exceeds our skill, the result is anxiety, as shown in Figure 5-3. A novice chef faced with the preparation of an entire banquet will be understandably anxious. If, on the other hand, our skill exceeds the challenge, the result is boredom. The master chef forced to make toast all day soon will become bored.

If skill and challenge are more or less evenly matched, however, the result is what Csikszentmihalyi calls "flow," the state of being totally engrossed in the experience. Experiences that provide flow are the experiences we tend to do for their own sake. Ronald Gross, in his book, *Peak Learning,* calls the anxiety state the "groan zone" and the boredom state the "drone zone," as contrasted with the "flow zone."

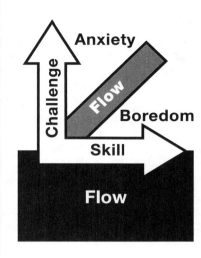

FIGURE 5-3   Flow.

Csikszentmihalyi and his fellow researchers have looked at many kinds of flow-producing experiences, from chess to rock climbing to surgery, and have identified eight "characteristic dimensions" of the flow experience:

1. Clear goals. An objective is distinctly defined, there is immediate feedback, and one knows instantly how well one is doing.

2. The opportunities for acting decisively are relatively high, and they are matched by one's perceived ability to act. In other words, personal skills are well suited to given challenges.

3. Action and awareness merge—"one-pointedness" of mind.

4. Concentration on the task at hand. Irrelevant stimuli disappear from consciousness, and worries and concerns are suspended temporarily.

5. A sense of potential control.

6. Loss of self-consciousness, transcendence of ego boundaries, a sense of growth and of being part of some greater entity.

7. Altered sense of time, which usually seems to pass faster.

8. Experience becomes autotelic. If several of the previous conditions are present, what one does becomes autotelic, or worth doing for its own sake.

The planning stage of the five-stage process gives you dimension 1—clear goals. By the time you start your quick and dirty draft, you have a clearly defined objective for that draft, as well as a clear set of criteria to use during the revising stage. The fact that writing begins with a blank page gives you dimension 2—the opportunity for acting decisively by using the best of your skills. The law of the next action provides dimensions 3 and 4—"one-pointedness" of mind and concentration on the task at hand. By dividing your writing process into 12 distinctive steps, you can focus intently on each one as you move through it; at the drafting stage, for example, you focus only on getting words down, not on getting them right. Together, these dimensions 3 and 4 can get you to dimensions 6 and 7—a loss of self-consciousness and an altered sense of time. By the end of your 10-minute drafting exercise, you may have already experienced these dimensions. If you've taken time in step 1 to define yourself as a "writer," you'll have achieved dimension 5—a sense of potential control.

In all, therefore, a five-stage writing process can make writing an autotelic experience for you—a "flow" experience that can be enjoyed for its own sake.

MANAGE YOUR WRITING *TODAY*

In this chapter's exercise, you practiced quick and dirty drafting—drafting without editing. Now it's time to do it for real.

- On the very next writing job you have to do, begin with some writing management: Remind yourself that you're a writer, that writing can be managed, and that it's largely a matter of managing time. Set up blocks of time for planning, drafting, and revising—with more time allocated for planning and revising than for drafting.

- Then begin the planning stage by "finding the 'we.'" Take perhaps five minutes to ask yourself, "What is the smallest community to which my audience and I both belong?" and "How are my audience and I alike and different in the four PACK dimensions: personality, attitude, circumstances, and knowledge?" Then take another five minutes to "make holes, not drills" by defining the purpose of the piece of writing. Ask yourself, "Is my purpose to tell my reader(s) about something, ask my reader(s) to do something, or both? Will this piece of writing function as conversation, correspondence, covenant, or conception—or some combination of those?" Take another five minutes or so to "get your stuff together," to gather information for the piece of writing. Use the reporter's checklist, my four pairs, or both. Go to resources, human and written, for the external information you need, and do brainstorming or mind-mapping for the information you already have in your head. Then end the planning stage with five minutes of "getting your ducks in a row," organizing your information to best achieve your purpose for your reader(s).

- Now "do it wrong the first time." Draft your document with as little editing as possible. Consider turning off your computer monitor as you do so.

Remember horror writer Stephen King's admonishment that "Only God gets it right the first time."

- Then take a break.
- When you come back from the break, revise your document.

When you've finished, take a few minutes to evaluate how the process worked for you. Evaluate especially whether "doing it wrong the first time" resulted in a more effective piece of writing at the end.

As Bradley S. Hayden of Western Michigan University has said, "Drafts are like newly born children: We can't expect them to go to graduate school when they are only a few days old. The most important thing is for them to have arrived into the world safely."

C H A P T E R

TAKE A BREAK AND CHANGE HATS

MANAGE YOUR INTERNAL WRITER AND EDITOR

I**N THE INTRODUCTION** to this book you learned the importance of improving your written products by improving your writing process. Specifically, you learned the importance of becoming a five-stage writer. In Chapters 1 through 4 you learned specific tools for the planning stage of the process. In Chapter 5, you drafted.

Now, as shown in Figure 6-1, you've come to what may be the most important stage in the writing process—the "down" time, the time you're not writing. Although you may have trouble justifying this to your boss or to your spouse, it's true. This important stage is the time between drafting and revising when you should get away from your writing—for minutes, for hours, or (if possible) for days. It's the time to take a break and change hats. We professional business writers—especially we older ones—even have a technical term for this stage. We call it "Miller Time."

BREAKING FOR OBJECTIVITY

Let's take the two parts of this chapter's title one part at a time. First is "Take a Break."

FIGURE 6-1   Take a break and change hats.

The reason for taking a break after drafting is that it can give you the "distance"—the objectivity—that you need to do good revision. Objectivity is important for at least three reasons.

The first, and most basic, reason is that objectivity lets you see what you wrote, not what you may have meant to write. Ask any writing teacher or trainer, and he or she will confirm the fact that many developing writers will look at their draft and literally read what they intended to say, not what they actually said. Once I worked with a writer who read aloud to me a sentence from his draft four times before realizing his mistake, exclaiming, "Duh!" and reading the sentence the way it was written on the page. You can't revise something until you've actually seen it.

The second reason is that objectivity will help you to see the document as the reader will see it. In 1751, the Earl of Chesterfield advised his son, "Read every paragraph after you have written it, in the critical view of discovering whether it is possible that any one man can mistake the true sense of it: and correct it accordingly."

The memo in Chapter 4 about the use of fluorescent paint in parking lots was easily understandable by the writer. She knew exactly what she wanted to say. Even if she had not organized it more carefully at the planning stage, she could have reorganized it at the revising stage if she had gotten some distance from it and read it from her reader's point of view. Before we revise a draft, we need to read it as if for the first time—the way our reader(s) will encounter it.

The third, and perhaps most important, reason for objectivity is that it can help us to overcome our own egos. Even if we don't think of ourselves as good writers, we feel close to the bad writing we've done. We don't want to accept criticism, even from ourselves.

Once we've written a draft, we've invested quite a bit of time and effort in it. Thus, as Rabbi Israel Salanter has said, "Writing is one of the easiest things; erasing is one of the hardest." We're reluctant to admit, even to ourselves, that something we've drafted might benefit from being changed.

Have you ever had the experience of reading a piece of writing that you did as a child or adolescent? Perhaps you've found old school papers, or love letters, or a diary. In my own experience, reading my oldest writing is both embarrassing and fun—fun because the writing sounds as if it were written by a totally different person. And of course, it was.

In business, of course, we don't have the luxury of waiting 10, 20, or 30 years to read our draft again. So we have to force ourselves to get something of the same kind of distance, the same kind of objectivity. Even in five minutes we can trick ourselves. We can print out our quick and dirty draft, set it down without reading it, and head for the restroom, vending machine, or coffee pot. When we return, we can say to ourselves, "Oh, there's that sales letter I've been putting off writing. Look! Someone must have drafted it for me! Hmm, let me read it. Well, it's not bad—but it's certainly not up to my standards yet. I'm not willing to put my name on it now. But at least it's been written! All I have to do is revise it until it's good enough for my signature."

Remember: The draft is a prototype. It's not a finished product. It's raw material.

In a way, writing is like poker. In poker, it's important not to think of any of the money in the pot as your money. If you put $10 in the pot before the draw, you just have to forget that fact. If, after the draw, you keep thinking of that $10, you'll be betting to protect your investment. And you'll make bad decisions. There's even a phrase from poker that we use in many other circumstances: "Don't throw good money after bad."

I'm certainly not here to teach you how to play poker. I'm here to teach you to write more effectively. But the principle is the same. If you think of the time and effort you've invested in a piece of writing, you're bound to be reluctant to change anything. To be an effective business writer, however, you simply have to lose that reluctance. As poet John Berryman said, "One must be ruthless with one's own writing or someone else will be."

When I say take a five-minute break out of a typical writing hour, that's the minimum. To the extent that you can control your time, if you have two days to do a one-hour piece of writing, complete your planning and drafting stages the first day, and save your revising until the second day. Sports agent Mark H. McCormack reminds us that "whenever President Harry Truman wrote an angry letter, he would put it away in his desk for 24 hours to see if he felt the same way the next day." Even with nonangry documents, a 24-hour break can be hugely valuable.

And if you have a week, putting four days between drafting and revising almost certainly will make your document even stronger. And if you're lucky enough to have more time than that, use it! For example, I'm drafting this chapter in June. I literally won't look at it again until August, a few weeks before the deadline for this book.

There's one more important strategy for getting the objectivity you need to revise effectively. I've been talking so far about the value of pretending that someone else wrote the draft. What if someone else really did? Please consider setting up an underground, subversive writing team in which you and a coworker routinely revise each other's drafts. You'll both end up writing better—and looking better.

FROM WRITER-BASED TO READER-BASED

One phenomenon that often happens when writers take a break and become more objective about their drafts is that they move from what theorist Linda Flower calls "writer-based" writing to what she calls "reader-based" writing. Writer-based writing is simply a record of the writer's own thought, with no concessions to the needs of a reader.

For an example of writer-based writing, read these paragraphs, from a memo from the vice president for personnel at one of my client companies, a large insurance firm:

> I received the results from the Spring examinations. I want to extend my congratulations to you for your success in passing Parts I & II. I know that to achieve this success took a special effort on your part.
>
> I am pleased that you are interested in your personal development and have taken the initiative to improve your knowledge of the insurance business and to increase your value to the company.

This is not bad for a quick and dirty draft. But when the vice president took a break and looked at the draft objectively, he realized that the memo was very writer-based. Each of its four sentences had *I* as its grammatical subject, as if the most important information in the message was that the vice president thought and felt something. Such self-centeredness doesn't necessarily reveal a massive ego problem; it's actually quite typical of first drafts.

Although such writer-centered writing is usually not effective at getting things done, Flower believes that it may be a necessary step in the writing process. Writers, she says, may need to first get words on paper (or on a computer screen) and only then shape them to meet the reader's needs. Here's how the vice president reshaped the memo to change its emphasis:

Congratulations on passing Parts I & II of the Spring examinations. Your success reflects a special effort on your part.

Your interest in your personal development and the initiative to improve your knowledge of the insurance business certainly increase your value to the company.

Though these sentences still could use some revision, they certainly show an effective move from writer-based to reader-based prose.

In the drafting stage, even with good planning, language may be spun out from the writer's mind organically, like silk from a silkworm. Before the revising stage can start, that language needs to become objective, like silk thread that can be woven into something beautiful, like a scarf, or useful, like a parachute.

This "weaving" process requires a special kind of double vision. On one hand, the writer must see the written document as a whole, just as a silk weaver must see the overall pattern of the fabric emerging from the loom. But the writer also must see the document as a collection of individual parts that can be manipulated, just as the weaver must concentrate on the individual threads of the warp and woof. Weavers seem to have no problem achieving this double vision, nor do architects, thinking both of grand sweeps of space and of individual beams and panes of glass. Yet we writers often have trouble seeing our work in this dual fashion.

One reason lies in economics. Unlike weavers or architects, we writers generate our material out of ourselves, so we come to value it as we would a child—and a child born of an especially hard labor. Moreover, we writers know instinctively the almost infinite power of the written word—the power, as mentioned in the introduction, of creating a reality. Words, to us, become almost sacred, priceless things.

Yet, to be good writers, we also must come to regard words as cheap, among the cheapest commodities on earth. We must know that the writing of a word takes only a second or two and a fraction of a penny's worth of electricity or ink—and that erasing that word costs even less. And we must be willing to do that erasing, that total destruction of language, without even a flicker of regret. In short, we must learn not to undervalue—or overvalue—the written word.

A *Time* article, in lamenting "The Decline of Editing," quoted writer John McPhee: "There are a lot of books around that smell of the tape recorder. Writing is so difficult that if a writer is looking at words on paper, say the transcript of a tape recording, it's damn difficult to resist them." The result, claims McPhee, is wordiness: "A lot of books go on too long because [the writer] recorded too much."

We can all learn from novelist and playwright Thornton Wilder. "An incinerator," he said, "is a writer's best friend."

THE TWO HATS

The second part of this chapter's title is "Change Hats." This is so because we businesspeople wear two hats when we write. And trying to wear both at the same time keeps us from writing as powerfully as we could.

You see, two different mental activities are involved in the writing process. When we write, two different kinds of things are happening. (I'll sometimes refer to them as two different parts of the brain, although that's not exactly true.)

One of these activities—occupying a big part of the brain—is the unbelievably complex job of converting ideas into hand movements. Think for a moment about what a complicated activity that is. You're at your computer, writing up your travel expenses and remembering the blue sedan you rented at O'Hare to get you around town. Your brain moves some muscles in the middle finger of your left hand, then the little finger, and then the index finger. The word *car* appears on the screen.

I think of that part of my brain as a tough-guy big-city reporter from black-and-white B movies of 1930s, 1940s, and 1950s, able to pound out an article at a moment's notice—the hard-boiled newsman who says, "Give me the story, chief, and I'll do it." I call that part of my brain my *Internal Writer,* in a rumpled fedora with a "Press" card in the hatband.

But psychologists tell us that another mental activity is also involved. It occupies the part of your brain that remembers the sedan and knows where you put the charge slip. It's the part that knows how expense reports look and what you can include in them. It's the part that also knows all those grammar and punctuation rules.

I think of that part of my brain as a crusty old newspaper editor from those same movies, yelling out assignments to his staff and grabbing the pencil from behind his ear to slash up the stories they submit. I call that part of my brain my *Internal Editor*, in a green eyeshade.

Now imagine that you're a newspaper reporter on your first day at work. Your boss gives you a "wire" story, from the Associated Press, and asks you to rewrite it. You sit down at your keyboard and start writing your first sentence. Suddenly you hear your boss's voice over your shoulder—and it's not in your imagination. "What a lousy way to start a story," he says.

"How do you want me to start it?" you ask him.

"That's your job," he replies. "But you sure haven't done it well so far."

You backspace over the three or four words you've written and start again. This time you get to the sixth or seventh word before your boss interrupts you again. "Don't they teach you people to spell anymore?" he says. "It's *i* before *e* except after *c*."

"Oh, that's right," you reply, and fix the error.

And so on. This bozo stands behind you as you write the entire story, sometimes correcting your grammar, sometimes criticizing your word choice, and sometimes fixing your punctuation.

Who could work under such conditions?

But that's what all of us do to ourselves at least some of the time. As one-stage writers (as shown in Figure 6-2), we wear both the writer's fedora and the editor's eyeshade at the same time. As we write a letter, memo, or report, our Internal Writer has to work very hard to coordinate the muscles that form the words. But at the same time that it's doing that, it also has to listen to our Internal Editor hassling it about every word and every sentence.

And nobody hassles us like our Internal Editor does. It's had great teachers: our parents, all our teachers, all our bosses. In fact, our Internal Editor is precisely those parents, teachers, and bosses preserved intact in our minds long after they've left our lives. As we write, that inner voice is always there, word by word, sentence by sentence, making us insecure about what we're saying and how we're saying it.

In short, as we write, our Internal Writer and Internal Editor are locked in a struggle for available time and resources. And that struggle—as first one is in control and then the other—wastes time. In fact, a 2001 University of Michigan study found that workers waste 20 to 40 percent of their productivity by "task switching," readjusting mentally as they move from one kind of activity to another.

We sometimes may feel that the only way to stop that internal conflict is to do what Raymond has done in Figure 6-3.

A better solution, though, is to do what real writers and editors do. A good newspaper editor makes the best assignment he can and then gets out

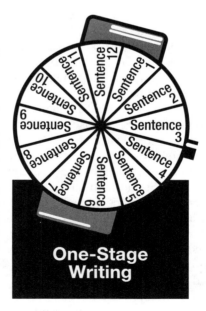

FIGURE 6-2   One-stage writing.

FIGURE 6-3   Raymond puts a stop to his critical inner dialogue.

of the way. A good editor lets a writer be a writer, doing a writer's job without interference. Only when a draft has been written does the editor come back on the scene to review and revise.

Good writers and good editors work separately. By doing that, they each do their own job better. And the same is true of the Internal Writer and the Internal Editor. Accomplished writers keep their Internal Writer and Internal Editor separate. They wear one hat at a time.

Writer Natalie Goldberg gives good advice: "It is important to separate the creator and the editor or internal censor. . . . If the editor is absolutely annoying . . . sit down whenever you need to and write what the editor is saying: give it full voice— 'You are a jerk, who ever said you could write, I hate your work, you suck. I'm embarrassed, you have nothing valuable to say, and besides, you can't spell. . . .' Sound familiar?"

"The more clearly you know the editor," she continues, "the better you can ignore it. After a while, like the jabbering of an old drunk fool, it becomes just prattle in the background."

Now you know why the five-stage writing process works. So far in the course you've just had to take my word for its value. Now you've learned the psychology behind it.

When you have a writing job to do, wear one hat at a time. Before you let your Internal Writer go to work, demand that your Internal Editor make the most complete assignment possible. In other words, use your Internal Editor to go through the planning stage of the writing process (shown again in Figure 6-4), following the steps covered so far in this course:

1. *Find the "We."* Identify the community to which you and your reader both belong. Consider the ways you and your reader are alike and different in the PACK dimensions: personality, attitude, circumstances, and knowledge.
2. *Make Holes, Not Drills.* Establish the purpose of your writing. Are you writing conversation, correspondence, covenant, or conception? Are you writing to tell your reader about something, to ask your reader to do something, or both?
3. *Get Your Stuff Together.* Gather the information that you want to include in the letter, memo, or report. Decide how much goes in and how much stays out.
4. *Get Your Ducks in a Row.* Determine the order in which your reader should get your information. What should come first? Second? Last?

At this point, your Internal Editor will have an incredibly detailed assignment to give to your Internal Writer: "I want you to write for this reader, for this purpose, using these materials, in this order. And here are a lot of details about each." Don't you feel more confident about your work

FIGURE 6-4   Five-stage writing.

when your boss tells you more clearly what she wants? Well, by going through a good planning stage, that's what you can do for yourself.

When your Internal Editor has made a complete assignment, then get him out of the way so that your Internal Writer can draft without interference. This is easier said than done, of course. With practice, however, you can learn to turn off your Internal Editor while you produce the quick and dirty drafts recommended in Chapter 5. As the title of that chapter said, you can learn to give yourself permission to "Do It Wrong the First Time."

If the 10-minute nonstop writing exercise in Chapter 5 was hard for you, you can now see why. Your Internal Editor kept trying to horn in.

The break stage recommended in this chapter is your opportunity to change hats again. After a break, the Internal Editor can come back into the room and read the draft as if someone else wrote it—because, in a way, someone else did.

Obviously, this distinction somewhat oversimplifies the matter. At the planning and revising stages, your Internal Editor sometimes needs to call on your Internal Writer to make notes (at the planning stage) or to actually make the changes (at the revising stage). In general, though, you can learn to wear one hat at a time. As newsman Don Marquis once said, "I never think when I write; nobody can do two things at the same time and do them well."

EXERCISE

The following questions will test your understanding of this chapter. The final examination for this course will include similar questions.

1. At what stage of the writing process should you decide the order in which you will present your main points?

   a. Managing

   b. Planning

   c. Drafting

   d. Revising

2. At what stage of the writing process should you make sure a word is spelled correctly?

   a. Managing

   b. Planning

   c. Drafting

   d. Revising

3. At what stage of the writing process should you decide between two words with approximately the same meaning?

   a. Managing

   b. Planning

   c. Drafting

   d. Revising

4. At what stage of the writing process should you put sentences down on paper or on a computer screen?

   a. Managing

   b. Planning

   c. Drafting

   d. Revising

5. At what stage of the writing process should you determine the purpose of your writing?

   a. Managing

   b. Planning

   c. Drafting

   d. Revising

6. At what stage of the writing process should you allocate time for the other stages in the process?

   a. Managing

   b. Planning

   c. Drafting

   d. Revising

7. At what stage of the writing process should you get a general idea of how to start and end the piece of writing?

   a. Managing

   b. Planning

   c. Drafting

   d. Revising

8. At what stage of the writing process should you review a paragraph to see if it has enough transition words?

   a. Managing

   b. Planning

   c. Drafting

   d. Revising

9. At what stage of the writing process should you get an initial sense of your audience?

   a. Managing

   b. Planning

   c. Drafting

   d. Revising

10. At what stage of the writing process should you collect any information you need for the writing?

   a. Managing

   b. Planning

   c. Drafting

   d. Revising

MANAGE YOUR WRITING *TODAY*

On the very next writing job you have to do, begin with some writing management: Remind yourself that you're a writer, that writing can be managed, and that it's largely a matter of managing time. Set up blocks of time for planning, drafting, and revising—with more time allocated for planning and revising than for drafting.

- Then call in your Internal Editor to make the best possible "assignment" for this writing task. Begin by spending five minutes "finding the 'we.'" Take another five minutes to ask yourself, "What is the smallest community to which my audience and I both belong?" and "How are my audience and I alike and different in the four PACK dimensions: personality, attitude, circumstances, and knowledge?" Spend another five minutes to "make holes, not drills" by defining the purpose of the piece of writing. Take another five minutes or so to "get your stuff together," to gather information for the piece of writing. Then end the planning stage with five minutes of "getting your ducks in a row," organizing your information to best achieve your purpose for your reader(s).

- Now "do it wrong the first time." Bring in your Internal Writer to draft your document with as little interference as possible from your Internal Editor.

- Then take a break—for as long as you can but for at least five minutes. Use this time to gain some objectivity about your draft and to "change hats" from your Internal Writer's rumpled fedora to your Internal Editor's eyeshade.

- When you return from the break, try to trick yourself into thinking that someone else wrote the draft, and look at it as if you're seeing it for the first time. Then revise your document using all the tools you already have in your toolbox.

When you've finished, take a few minutes to evaluate how the process worked for you. Evaluate especially whether "taking a break and changing hats" resulted in a more effective piece of writing at the end.

SIGNAL YOUR TURNS
MANAGE YOUR PARAGRAPHS

ENTREPRENEUR AND writer Peter Hay tells a story about Sam Cherr, cofounder of the great advertising agency Young & Rubicam. According to the story, Cherr required all marketing plans to be written in considerable detail. A young employee once brought such a plan, in the 200-page range, to Cherr. After several days of no response, the employee went to Cherr's office and asked what he thought of the plan. Cherr replied, "Is this the best you can do?"

The employee admitted that he probably could do better, so he took back the plan. After extensive rewriting, he resubmitted the 200 pages. Again, he waited in vain and finally asked Cherr's opinion. Again, Cherr responded, "Is this the best you can do?"

Disappointed again, the employee confessed that yes, he probably could do better. After a weekend of rewriting, he again submitted the plan. When, several days later, he hadn't heard back from Cherr, he again asked him what he thought. For a third time, Cherr replied, "Is this the best you can do?"

This time, the young employee gulped and confessed, "Yes, Mr. Cherr, that's the best I can do."

"In that case," said Sam Cherr, "I'll read it."

The story tells the truth that good writing depends on good revising. To many of us, this truth comes as a surprise. Because we don't think of writing as a process that can be managed like any other business process, we imagine that "good" writers produce good writing the first time and therefore don't have to revise. We may even have memories from grade school, when *rewrite* was a bad word, something we had to do when we didn't write well enough at first, something that kept us in from recess.

In fact, some research shows that good writers revise more, not less, than ordinary writers. Historian Paul Fussell once reported, "Crappy work I do twice, good work I do three times." American novelist John Dos Passos raised the bar even higher when he said, "I do a lot of revising. Certain chapters six or seven times."

Despite the difficulty, many professional writers take great pleasure in revising their drafts. Playwright Neil Simon, for example, has written, "In baseball, you only get three swings and you're out. In rewriting, you get almost as many swings as you want and you know, sooner or later, you'll hit the ball."

TOOLS FOR REVISION

With this chapter, as Figure 7-1 shows, we move into the revising stage of the writing process. Despite some of the quotations you've just read, revising doesn't have to take forever. In a typical one-hour writing job, revision really can be done effectively in 20 to 30 minutes.

To revise effectively, we need tools. This chapter and the next four provide such tools. Before we get to them, however, we need to make three points about revision tools:

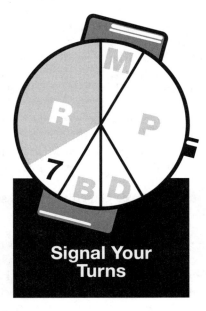

FIGURE 7-1   Signal your turns.

1. Revision tools are not drafting tools.
2. Revision tools are not rules.
3. You already have most of the revision tools you need.

Let's look closely at each of these three points. First, the tools you'll learn in this book are tools for revision, not tools for drafting. This is important. When you learn new tools for improving your writing, your Internal Editor inevitably will try to get you to use those tools at the drafting stage. With each new tool, your Internal Editor will have one more thing to hassle your Internal Writer about as you draft.

I read once about a "psych-out" technique to use if you're playing tennis against a tough opponent. After watching your opponent warm up, you say to him, "As I've been watching you, I've finally realized how to improve my backhand. It's the way you hold your thumb. How do you do that exactly?"

Unless your opponent is on to you, he probably will say, "Gee, I don't know. I've never thought about it."

"Well, think about," you say. "I'd really appreciate any advice from you."

Then you start the match. If your opponent has fallen in your trap, he will be thinking about his thumb, perhaps for the first time. Your opponent will focus on that thumb—not on the ball, not on the net, not on the lines of the court. And this fact may give you the edge you need.

That's how your Internal Editor works. Like your tennis opponent, your inner editorial voice may well concentrate on the most recent thing it has paid attention to. So please, please remember that the powerful tools you'll learn in Chapters 7 through 11 are revising tools, not drafting tools.

Second, keep in mind the important difference between tools and rules. When we all first learned to write, we were taught a number of rules for better writing. Some of those rules really were rules, and this book will enforce them in Chapter 11 when we "finish" our writing. Other so-called rules, however, were just teaching devices—or even teaching folklore—important only in limited cases or at certain stages in our development as writers. These include such "rules" as "Don't begin sentences with *and*," "Don't use *I* or *you* in your writing," and "Don't end sentences with prepositions."

Most of the lessons you'll be learning in these five chapters are not rules but tools. Rules say, "Do this. Don't do that." Tools say, "If you want to achieve this, then maybe you'll want to do that." Rules control you; tools help you to take control. As Thomas Edison once said, "Hell, there are no rules here. We're trying to accomplish something."

These next five chapters, then, are designed to show you how to take more control of your writing at the revising stage of your writing process. These chapters emphasize that you don't have to use the first words, sentences, or paragraphs that occur to you—those that come as you write your draft. Instead, you can take charge of those words, sentences, and paragraphs and make them work for you.

The third point is that you already have most of the tools you need to revise effectively. As the introduction to this book suggested, you've acquired these tools by all the reading you've done in your life. If, for some reason, you stop reading this book right now, you'll already have become a better reviser just by having learned to revise not while you draft but after you draft. The tools you already have will have become even more useful to you as you use them at a separate revision stage.

The additional tools in these five chapters have been selected carefully both because they're especially effective and because most of the writers I work with have not learned them before. In effect, the truth is that you already have a pretty good basic tool kit—perhaps a hammer, a saw, screwdrivers, and pliers. I simply want to add to it by giving you, say, a socket wrench set and a power drill.

TURN SIGNALS

The late Malcolm Forbes said it best: "People who read business letters are as human as thee and me. Reading a letter shouldn't be a chore."

This is our job as writers—making the act of reading as easy as possible so that our readers can give all their attention to what we are saying. At the revising stage of our writing process, we need to make sure that our writing "flows," moving the reader smoothly from one sentence to the next.

Read the following paragraph. I think you'll agree that it doesn't flow. The sentences seem "choppy," with awkward changes of direction. The writer seems unsure about where she is going. The paragraph, in fact, isn't really a paragraph at all, just a collection of disconnected sentences. Reading it is, in Forbes's words, a chore.

> The next sample, Formula D-7, is an excellent adhesive. It was the strongest of any tested. It was one of the most water-resistant. It has several disadvantages. Its cost is fairly high. Its viscosity would perhaps require new application equipment. Its viscosity would perhaps require modifications in existing equipment. Its storage-temperature requirements are rather strict. In my judgment, these disadvantages are outweighed by its overall quality. I recommend that Formula D-7 be used for the project.

One important way to improve the readability of such writing—to make it less of a chore for your reader—is by using "turn signals," words or phrases that show the relationship of each sentence with a previous one.

Pretend that you and I work together and that our work team has planned a picnic on a Saturday morning. We're going to bring our families and meet in the company parking lot. Then I'm going to lead the "convoy" of cars out to a great picnic spot I know in the country.

It would really help you if I used turn signals. Without turn signals, you wouldn't be prepared for the turns I make. You might, in fact, become as exasperated as Jason in Figure 7-2. With turn signals, I'd be much easier to follow.

For exactly the same reason, the written "turn signals" we'll be talking about in this chapter make it easier for the reader to follow the writer through a memo, letter, or report. (Note that we already use the word *follow* when we talk about reading a piece of writing.)

To signal our turns in a piece of writing, we need to understand something about the relationships that sentences can have with each other. One authority on writing, Ross Winterowd, has listed six kinds of relationships that can exist between sentences, each with its own—in my words—turn signals. These six relationships are listed in Figure 7-3. Each of these relationships has its own turn signals.

The first relationship can be signaled by the word *and*. Two sentences have an *and* relationship when the second sentence simply adds more information of the same kind. An *and* relationship therefore is like a plus sign in mathematics. Besides the word *and*, this relationship can be signaled with such words and phrases as these:

- also
- too

FIGURE 7-2 Jason brings a note of sarcasm to his driver critiques.

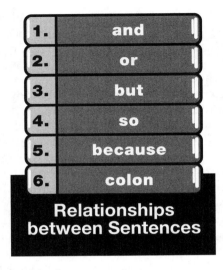

FIGURE 7-3   Relationships between sentences.

- moreover
- furthermore
- in addition
- next
- second
- third

And relationships can also be signaled by numbers or bullets in a list—like the list you just read. Such lists are extremely helpful to readers. One study of Web-based writing found that the use of headings and bullets increases usability by 47 percent.

Here's that sample paragraph again, this time with its sentences numbered so that we can refer to them more easily:

(1) The next sample, Formula D-7, is an excellent adhesive. (2) It was the strongest of any tested. (3) It was one of the most water-resistant. (4) It has several disadvantages. (5) Its cost is fairly high. (6) Its viscosity would perhaps require new application equipment. (7) Its viscosity would perhaps require modifications in existing equipment. (8) Its storage-temperature requirements are rather strict. (9) In my judgment, these disadvantages are outweighed by its overall quality. (10) I recommend that Formula D-7 be used for the project.

In this paragraph, the second and third sentences have an *and* relationship. The advantage cited in sentence 3 is meant to be *added,* in our reader's mind, to the advantage cited in sentence 2:

It was the strongest of any tested. It was one of the most water-resistant.

To signal this relationship to our reader, we can add the word *and* after the second sentence; then (as a bonus) we can eliminate the repeated words *It was* and combine the two sentences:

It was the strongest of any tested and one of the most water-resistant.

The next possible relationship usually is signaled by the word *or.* Two sentences have an *or* relationship when they present alternatives. Besides the word *or*, this relationship can be signaled with the words *alternatively* and *otherwise.*

Sentences 6 and 7, the two "viscosity" sentences, have an *or* relationship expressing alternative ways of solving a problem:

Its viscosity would perhaps require new application equipment. Its viscosity would perhaps require modifications in existing equipment.

We can make things easier for our reader by adding the word *or* between the sentences and by deleting the words *Its viscosity would perhaps require,* the second time they are used:

Its viscosity would perhaps require new application equipment or modifications in existing equipment.

Once we have combined these two "viscosity" sentences, we now have a series of three sentences—including sentences 5 and 8—about disadvantages of the adhesive. These sentences all have an *and* relationship, so we can make them into a series using the word *and:*

Its cost is fairly high, its viscosity would perhaps require new application equipment or modifications in existing equipment, and its storage-temperature requirements are rather strict.

Although this is a fairly long sentence, it's easier to read than the three disconnected sentences we had before. (Of course, we could make the three disadvantages into a bulleted list as another way of signaling their *and* relationship. In this particular paragraph, however, we may not want to call attention to the disadvantages in this way.)

The third relationship between sentences can be signaled by the word *but.* Two sentences have a *but* relationship when the second sentence partially contradicts, contradicts, or qualifies the first. Besides the word *but*, this relationship can be signaled with such words and phrases as these:

- however
- nevertheless
- nonetheless
- on the other hand

One *but* relationship occurs before sentence 4:

It has several disadvantages.

This sentence contradicts, or at least qualifies, the previous sentences, which were about advantages. So we can help our reader by adding a *but* turn signal to this sentence. For example, we could say, "It nevertheless has several disadvantages."

Similarly, sentence 9, the sentence beginning, "In my judgment," has a *but* relationship with its preceding sentences. Those preceding sentences were about disadvantages, but now we're about to make a positive judgment. For variety, we might add the word *However* at the beginning of this sentence to signal the turn:

However, in my judgment, these disadvantages are outweighed by its overall quality.

The fourth and fifth possible relationships are really the same relationship seen from two different sides. Two sentences have a *so* relationship when the second expresses the result, conclusion, or effect of the first sentence. Besides the word *so*, this relationship can be signaled with such words and phrases as these:

- therefore
- thus
- for this reason

The *because* relationship is the opposite of the *so* relationship: Two sentences have a *because* relationship when the second gives the cause or reason for the first. Besides the word *because*, this relationship can be signaled with such words as *since* and *for*.

In the sample paragraph, sentences 9 and 10 have a *so* relationship. We might signal this relationship by adding the word *therefore* to the last sentence at any of several points near the beginning of that sentence.

However, in my judgment, these disadvantages are outweighed by its overall quality. I therefore recommend that Formula D-7 be used for the project.

The last relationship is often signaled with a punctuation mark, the *colon*. Two sentences have a *colon* relationship when the second sentence gives specifics for the generalization made in the first sentence. Beside a colon, this relationship can be signaled with such words and phrases as these:

- specifically
- for example
- to illustrate

Sentence 1 of the sample paragraph has a *colon* relationship with the combined sentence that follows it. The first sentence says that the adhesive is excellent; the next sentences give the specific ways it is excellent. So we can signal where we are going by adding a colon after that first sentence:

The next sample, Formula D-7, is an excellent adhesive: it was the strongest of any tested and one of the most water-resistant.

In the same way, the sentence reporting that the adhesive has several disadvantages has a *colon* relationship with the following series. Therefore, we can put a colon after that sentence as well:

It nevertheless has several disadvantages: its cost is fairly high, its viscosity would perhaps require new application equipment or modifications in existing equipment, and its storage-temperature requirements are rather strict.

The following paragraph shows the result of adding all these turn signals—and, as a by-product, deleting some repeated words. I hope you agree that it's a much-improved paragraph. Naturally, this particular information could be presented in other ways: in a table, for example. However, whenever you're writing sentences, you can use turn signals to make your writing much easier to read:

The next sample, Formula D-7, is an excellent adhesive: it was the strongest of any tested and one of the most water-resistant. It nevertheless has several disadvantages: its cost is fairly high, its viscosity would perhaps require new application equipment or modifications in existing equipment, and its storage-temperature requirements are rather strict. However, in my judgment, these disadvantages are outweighed by its overall quality. I therefore recommend that Formula D-7 be used for the project.

One final note: If you go back now and read the original paragraph, you may find that it looks better to you than you first thought. This is so because you now know where it's going. You don't need as many turn signals.

This is the position you're always in when you read your *own* drafts. Because you know where you're going, you may not feel a need for turn signals. But turn signals aren't for you. They're for the person following you.

Bill Jensen, in his book *Simplicity*, expresses this issue well: "When people are *in need of* communication, they want others to take the time to listen, and then to take the time to create meaning, clarity, and connections between ideas. But when they have to *do the communicating*, saving time becomes a priority. . . . When it comes to communication, business is facing major discipline and accountability problems. It's like the line about change: Taking the time to create clarity is important—as long as it's the other guy who has to do it."

Don't fall into this trap. Use turn signals even more than you think you need to. If you do, reading your memos, letters, and reports won't be as much of a chore.

EXERCISES

Exercise A

The following questions will test your understanding of this chapter. The final examination for this course will include similar questions.

1. Which of the following shows the most effective use of turn signals?

    a. Capacity is more than 2.5 million barrels per day. Current production is much lower.

    b. Capacity is more than 2.5 million barrels per day, but current production is much lower.

    c. Capacity is more than 2.5 million barrels per day, and current production is much lower.

    d. Capacity is more than 2.5 million barrels per day, because current production is much lower.

2. Which of the following shows the most effective use of turn signals?

    a. The emirate produces liquefied natural gas. The emirate produces natural gas liquids.

    b. The emirate produces liquefied natural gas. However, the emirate produces natural gas liquids.

    c. The emirate produces liquefied natural gas and natural gas liquids.

    d. The emirate produces liquefied natural gas, but the emirate produces natural gas liquids.

3. Which of the following shows the most effective use of turn signals?

    a. NGL is produced in two plants. One is on Das Island. One is at Ruwais.

    b. NGL is produced in two plants. One is on Das Island, but one is at Ruwais.

    c. NGL is produced in two plants. Therefore, one is on Das Island. One is at Ruwais.

    d. NGL is produced in two plants: one is on Das Island and the other at Ruwais.

4. Which of the following shows the most effective use of turn signals?

    a. Some emirates have a corporate tax law, but it is applied only to foreign oil companies and foreign banks operating in those emirates.

    b. Some emirates have a corporate tax law. Therefore, it is applied only to foreign oil companies and foreign banks operating in those emirates.

    c. Some emirates have a corporate tax law. And it is applied only to foreign oil companies and foreign banks operating in those emirates.

    d. Some emirates have a corporate tax law, so it is applied only to foreign oil companies and foreign banks operating in those emirates.

5. Which of the following shows the most effective use of turn signals?

    a. The meeting was very beneficial, but new subjects were discussed.

    b. The meeting was very beneficial, so new subjects were discussed.

    c. The meeting was very beneficial because new subjects were discussed.

    d. The meeting was very beneficial; however, new subjects were discussed.

6. Which of the following shows the most effective use of turn signals?

    a. The subcommittee report did not arrive in time. It had to be mailed to participants later.

    b. The subcommittee report did not arrive in time, but it had to be mailed to participants later.

    c. The subcommittee report did not arrive in time, and it had to be mailed to participants later.

    d. The subcommittee report did not arrive in time, so it had to be mailed to participants later.

7. Which of the following shows the most effective use of turn signals?

    a. The report will cover traditional uses of LPG. It will cover use of LPG as an alternative transport fuel.

    b. The report will cover both traditional uses of LPG and its use as an alternative transport fuel.

    c. The report will cover traditional uses of LPG. However, it will cover uses of LPG as an alternative transport fuel.

    d. The report will cover traditional uses of LPG, but it will cover its uses as an alternative transport fuel.

8. Which of the following shows the most effective use of turn signals?

    a. The course will examine global supply and demand balances. The course will examine regional supply and demand balances.

    b. The course will examine global supply and demand balances, but it will examine regional supply and demand balances.

    c. The course will examine global supply and demand balances. The course also will examine regional supply and demand balances.

    d. The course will examine global and regional supply and demand balances.

9. Which of the following shows the most effective use of turn signals?

    a. The February meeting was canceled. Many participants would be unable to attend.

    b. The February meeting was canceled, and many participants would be unable to attend.

    c. The February meeting was canceled, but many participants would be unable to attend.

    d. The February meeting was canceled because many participants would be unable to attend.

10. Which of the following shows the most effective use of turn signals?

    a. The writing process has five stages. They are managing, planning, drafting, breaking, and revising.

    b. The writing process has five stages: managing, planning, drafting, breaking, and revising.

    c. The writing process has five stages. But they are managing, planning, drafting, breaking, and revising.

    d. The writing process has five stages. Therefore, they are managing, planning, drafting, breaking, and revising.

Exercise B

Revise the following memo, signaling turns more effectively and making any other changes that will improve it.

In the past, procedures for repair and calibration of test equipment have been unsatisfactory. Too much time has been spent taking instruments to Instrument Services. Employees have spent too much time picking equipment up from Instrument Services. Misplacement of some equipment has occurred.

On November 10 a new procedure will go into effect. "Drop zones" have been created for the pickup of test equipment. If you have instruments in need of calibration, take them to the appropriate drop zone in your building. Drop zones will be used for repair of instruments. Managers may consult the attached list for drop zone locations. Pickup will occur twice weekly. It will occur on Mondays and Thursdays.

Managers will be responsible for getting their equipment to the drop zone. They may send representatives to do it. Returns will be made by Instrument Services personnel. To ensure that instruments are returned to the correct manager, have the correct department and building number marked on each instrument before taking it to the drop zone.

Inquiries about whether an instrument has been repaired or calibrated should be directed to Instrument Services. Do not call the drop zone coordinator to find out if a piece of equipment is ready. Managers should call Instrument Services if they have any questions on the drop zone system.

MANAGE YOUR WRITING *TODAY*

On the very next writing job you have to do, begin with some writing management: Remind yourself that you're a writer, that writing can be managed, and that it's largely a matter of managing time. Set up blocks of time for planning, drafting, and revising—with more time allocated for planning and revising than for drafting.

- Then call in your Internal Editor to make the best possible "assignment" for this writing task. Begin by spending five minutes "finding the 'we.'" Take another five minutes to ask yourself, "What is the smallest community to which my audience and I both belong?" and "How are my audience and I alike and different in the four PACK dimensions: personality, attitude, circumstances, and knowledge?" Spend another five minutes to "make holes, not drills" by defining the purpose of the piece of writing. Take another five minutes or so to "get your stuff together," to gather information for the piece of writing. Then end the planning stage with five minutes of "getting your ducks in a row," organizing your information to best achieve your purpose for your reader(s).

- Now "do it wrong the first time." Bring in your Internal Writer to draft your document, with as little interference as possible from your Internal Editor.

- Then take a break—for as long as you can, but for at least five minutes. Use this time to gain some objectivity about your draft and to "change hats" from your Internal Writer's rumpled fedora to your Internal Editor's eyeshade.

- When you return from the break, try to trick yourself into thinking that someone else wrote the draft, and look at it as if you're seeing it for the first time. Then revise your document using all the tools you already have in your toolbox. However, pay special attention to "signaling your turns," guiding your reader from sentence to sentence.

When you've finished, take a few minutes to evaluate how the process worked for you. Evaluate especially whether using turn signals resulted in a more effective piece of writing at the end.

C H A P T E R

SAY WHAT YOU MEAN
MANAGE YOUR SUBJECTS AND VERBS

DANIEL **D**EFOE, **AUTHOR** of *Robinson Crusoe*, also wrote one of the first business how-to books in English, *The Complete English Tradesman*, published in 1745. In that book, Defoe wrote, "A tradesman's letters should be plain, concise, and to the purpose. . . . He that affects a rumbling and bombast style and fills his letter with compliments and flourishes makes a very ridiculous figure in trade."

After more than 250 years, Defoe's advice stills holds up. Like Connie in Figure 8-1, effective business writing gets to the point and says what it means. Specifically, it matches the structure of each sentence (what the sentence *says*) with the content of that sentence (what the sentence *means*).

As Figure 8-2 shows, we're now at the second step in the revising stage of the writing process. At this step we focus on managing sentence structure, especially the subjects and verbs of our sentences.

This is the first chapter that uses grammatical terms. But please don't worry if your knowledge of formal grammar is somewhat fuzzy. By the end of this chapter you'll have learned, through examples, all you need to know about verbs and subjects.

As you work your way through this chapter, remember the three points made at the beginning of Chapter 7:

1. Revision tools are not drafting tools.
2. Revision tools are not rules.
3. You already have most of the revision tools you need.

FIGURE 8-1   Connie always lets Glen know if she's happy.

Remember especially the first point. When you're drafting—"doing it wrong the first time"—you should not be worrying about grammar.

HIDDEN SUBJECTS

At this step in the revising stage, your main job is to check that most of your grammatical subjects and verbs are the *real* subjects and verbs of your sentences.

Let's begin with subjects. Look at the following sentence:

It is difficult to control costs.

The grammatical subject is *it*, but that's hardly the *real* subject, the noun or pronoun the sentence is about. The reader subconsciously tries to find meaning in that subject and comes up empty-handed.

The *real* subject of the sentence is *costs* or, perhaps, *control*, both "hidden" later in the sentence. The sentence can be improved by making the hidden, real subject also the grammatical subject. So consider revising the sentence to one of the following:

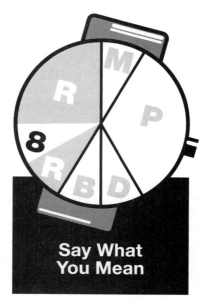

FIGURE 8-2   Say what you mean.

Costs are difficult to control.

or

Controlling costs is difficult.

When the reader reads the subject of either of these sentences, she knows what the sentence is about. The sentence says what it means.

One common place to find hidden subjects is in sentences beginning with *There*.

There needs to be more tribute paid to these unselfish workers.

The real subject of this sentence is not *There* but *tribute* or, perhaps even, *workers*. Depending on which of these nouns you want to emphasize, you could improve the sentence in either of two ways:

More tribute should be paid to these unselfish workers.

or

These unselfish workers deserve more tribute.

HIDDEN VERBS

Even more common than hidden subjects are hidden verbs. English has a tendency—no, English *tends*—to "nominalize"—to make verbs into nouns. *Tend*, for example, is a verb, but it is often changed into the noun *tendency*. Once you have made that change, you don't have a verb in your sentence any more, so you insert a "filler" verb such as *has, gives,* or *makes*:

He *tends* to be late.
He *has* a *tendency* to be late.

Ruth Walker, writing in *The Christian Science Monitor,* decries this phenomenon: "Look what's happening to verbs—the 'muscles' of language. They're being crowded out by more sedate linking-verb constructions. . . . 'He lost his job' often loses out to 'He became unemployed.' Instead of 'Ace Insurance Agency serves the maritime industry,' we often get, 'Ace is a provider of insurance services to the maritime industry.'"

With this in mind, look at this sentence:

The committee reached an agreement on the project.

The verb is *reached*, but this is not the *real* verb, the action that the committee performed. The committee didn't *reach;* it *agreed. Reached* is a filler verb; the real verb, *agree*, has been changed into the noun *agreement*. So consider revising the sentence to "The committee agreed on the project."

Here's a sentence from a report I once edited:

The consumer must make intelligent choices when buying tires.

The verb in this sentence is *make*. But is the consumer really making something? No. What the sentence *means* is that the consumer must *choose*. So we can improve this sentence by making it say what it means:

The consumer must choose intelligently when buying tires.

Alternatively, since the word *consumer* implies buying, we might revise the sentence even further:

The consumer must choose tires intelligently.

Here's another:

Ellen made a recommendation that we conduct a survey of employee morale.

This sentence has two clauses, each with its own verb: *made* and *conduct*. Both are empty filler verbs. In each clause the real action has been hidden in a noun: *recommendation* and *survey*. The sentence will be stronger if we turn those hidden verbs into real verbs:

Ellen recommended that we survey employee morale.

Writer and consultant Lee Wood offers a particularly good (bad?) example of a hidden verb. She once revised the following sentence:

Membership will be twice as much next year.

into:

Membership will double next year.

Don't you agree that the revised sentence is much stronger with the verb *double* replacing the verb *be*?

HIDDEN SUBJECTS *AND* VERBS

Pay special attention to sentences beginning with *It is*, *There is*, and *There are*. Such sentences often have neither the *real* subject nor the *real* verb in the subject and verb positions:

1. It is not until Wednesday that the parts will arrive.
2. There is a wide range of costs.
3. There are three reasons why you should expand the product line.

The grammatical subjects and verbs of all three sentences are absolutely empty.

In sentence 1, the real subject is *parts*, and the real verb is *arrive*. Consider revising it to, "The parts will arrive Wednesday" or "The parts will not arrive until Wednesday" (depending on whether you're the supplier, promising, or the buyer, complaining).

In business writing, the *It is* combination is so common that humorist Dave Barry makes fun of it in his book, *Claw Your Way to the Top:* "State that something is your understanding. This statement should be firm, vaguely disapproving, and virtually impossible to understand. A good standard one is: 'It is my understanding that this was to be ascertained in advance of any further action, pending review.'"

In sentence 2, the real subject is *costs*, and the real verb is *range*. Therefore, revise it to, "Costs range widely."

Novelist Philip Roth probably was referring to just this kind of revision when he wrote, "I turn sentences around. That's my life. I write a sentence and then I turn it around. Then I look at it and I turn it around again."

Often, as in sentence 3, you'll have a choice about which noun or pronoun in the sentence should be made the subject. If you want to emphasize the three reasons, make *reasons* the subject:

Three reasons why you should expand the product line are . . .

If you want to emphasize the reader, make *you* the subject:

You should expand the product line for three reasons.

If you want to emphasize the product line, make *line* the subject:

The product line should be expanded for three reasons.

Therefore, consider revising sentences such as "It is helpful to check subjects and verbs" to "Checking subjects and verbs helps." You'll be saying what you mean, and you'll be a more effective manager of your writing.

ACTIVE OR PASSIVE

As for verbs themselves, they generally are more readable and effective when they are active, not passive. Consider these sentences:

The book was ordered by us last week.
We ordered the book last week.

In the first sentence, the verb is passive: the subject (*book*) "receives" the action of the verb (*was ordered*). The second sentence is much more effective: the subject (*we*) is "doing" the acting, so the verb (*ordered*) is active.

To locate passive verbs, look for an action verb in its past participle form (usually ending in *–ed*), preceded by a form of the verb *to be* (*is, are, was, were, be, am*, or *been*). In most such cases, the person or thing doing the acting comes later in the sentence or is left out entirely. See whether you can improve the sentence by moving that word (or words) earlier, making it the subject of the sentence, and changing the verb into an active one.

At times, however, you will want to use a passive verb instead of an active one. For example, if the *real* subject of your sentence receives the action of the verb, then a passive verb may be more effective. In technical and scientific writing in particular, the real subject is often the passive recipient of procedures and tests:

The sample was heated to 500°C and subjected to Test B. The following changes were observed.

To put these sentences into active form ("I heated the sample. . . . I observed the following changes") would put far too much emphasis on the writer. So like other principles of revision you've learned in this course, changing verbs to their active forms is a tool, not a rule. Journalist William Safire, in his book *Fumblerules*, makes fun of people who preach that active verbs are always better. "The passive voice," he writes passively, "should never be used."

The tool of changing passive verbs to active verbs is a useful safeguard against the unthinking overuse of passive verbs, but it should not be applied when there is good reason for the passive voice.

One final note about passive verbs: They can be used to avoid taking responsibility. Notice the difference between "I made mistakes" and "Mistakes were made." Every politician prefers the latter, and every voter should see through it.

MODIFIERS

Pulitzer Prize winner J. Anthony Lukas once said, "If the noun is good and the verb is strong, you almost never need an adjective." Still, we can't do completely without modifiers—adjectives and adverbs.

To revise modifiers, it helps to understand something about how people read. Readers, as they move through a sentence, continually move words and phrases into memory. But memory is of two kinds, and knowing this fact can help you as you revise your sentences.

The two kids of memory, short term and long term, are like the short- and long-term parking lots at many airports. Short-term parking lots are close to the terminal and thus more convenient but are also smaller and more expensive. Long-term parking lots are larger and cheaper but more remote.

Short-term memory, too, is "closer" to the immediate perception of words on a page. As words are read, they are stored in short-term memory as words. But space in short-term memory is limited; some psychologists estimate its capacity at five to nine "items." Thus, as soon as individual words can be grouped together into meaningful units, they are moved "farther back" into long-term memory. Here they are stored not as words but as meanings. As an example, you almost certainly cannot remember now the exact wording of my paragraph comparing memory with parking lots. But you do remember (I hope) the paragraph's meaning.

One goal, then, of the revising stage should be to let the reader, as often as possible, combine words into larger meanings in order to transfer them into long-term memory. If this combining is delayed too long, the short-term memory becomes overloaded and thus emptied, and the reader must backtrack in the sentence to figure out what it's about.

And this brings us back to subjects and verbs. If too many modifiers separate the subject and verb, the short-term memory gets overloaded, and reading becomes difficult. Consider this sentence:

A new federal regulation regarding the sale of snack foods in competition with federally subsidized meal programs in schools is in effect this fall.

Here, the subject, *regulation*, must be held in suspension while a 14-word modifier goes by until the verb, *is*, comes along. The readability of this sentence can be improved greatly if the long modifier is postponed until after the verb. This keeps the subject and verb close enough together that they can be combined easily and moved quickly into long-term memory:

A new federal regulation is in effect this fall, a regulation regarding the sale of snack foods in competition with federally subsidized meal programs in schools.

Notice that the word *regulation* has been repeated to keep it close to the phrase that modifies it.

Here's another example from the same report:

In addition, the judge who ruled to uphold the regulation in two suits brought against the department said that the USDA could not exempt fortified foods from any of the restricted categories of food.

This sentence is more readable if revised like this:

In addition, in two suits brought against the department, the judge upholding the regulation said the USDA could not exempt fortified foods from any of the restricted categories of food.

The best place for modifiers is usually after the subject and verb. Extensive use of final modifiers, especially ones separated from the subject and verb by punctuation, is a relatively recent development in the English language but an extraordinarily valuable one. Francis Christensen, who first called this development to wide attention, labels sentences with separated final modifiers as "cumulative sentences." Here's an example:

The engineers concentrated their efforts on total efficiency, the highest possible ratio between energy-out and energy-in, not just on one or two isolated areas.

Such cumulative sentences have a powerful advantage for the reader: They require almost no suspension of words in short-term memory, almost no backtracking to pick up modifiers. The subject and verb come early ("The engineers concentrated"), and thus they can be combined into a single meaning and moved immediately into long-term memory. The subsequent modifiers refer to things that have been named already, and so they, too, can be moved quickly to long-term memory to join the things they modify. One key to creating effective, readable sentences is to stop thinking of sentences existing in space—on paper or on screen—and start thinking of your sentences as existing in time as a reader processes them.

A fringe benefit of cumulative sentences is that they are remarkably easy to write. As you begin revising your sentences into cumulative form, you'll find that more cumulative sentences will start coming out on their own at the drafting stage. When you write a cumulative sentence, you don't need to invent the entire sentence and hold it in your mind before you begin to write it. Instead, you can write your subject and verb, drop in a colon, dash, or comma, and then provide the details. That's just what the writer of this sentence did:

> I suggest a new advertising campaign, aimed not at our traditional teenage market but at the growing number of twenty- to-thirty-year-olds, a campaign emphasizing not glamour but economy.

EXERCISES

Exercise A

The following questions will test your understanding of this chapter. The final examination for this course will include similar questions.

1. Which of the following sentences manages subjects and verbs most effectively?

   a. It seems probable that we will be unable to participate.

   b. We probably can't participate.

   c. Our participation will not be probable.

   d. There is a low probability that we will be able to participate.

2. Which of the following sentences manages subjects and verbs most effectively?

   a. We need to understand the strategy better.

   b. We have a need to gain a better understanding of the strategy.

   c. We need to gain a better understanding of the strategy.

   d. We have a need to understand the strategy better.

3. Which of the following sentences manages subjects and verbs most effectively?

   a. I would like you to determine how such a process would be of benefit to us.

   b. Please make a determination of how such a process would be of benefit to us.

   c. Please determine how such a process would benefit us.

   d. I would like you to make a determination of how such a process would benefit us.

4. Which of the following sentences manages subjects and verbs most effectively?

   a. It is difficult to control total expenses.

   b. There is a difficulty in the control of total expenses.

   c. Total expenses are difficult to control.

   d. It is the case that total expenses are difficult to control.

5. Which of the following sentences manages subjects and verbs most effectively?

   a. It is my opinion that market segmentation issues are clear.

   b. It is my opinion that there is clarity in market segmentation issues.

   c. I believe that there is clarity in market segmentation issues.

   d. I believe that market segmentation issues are clear.

6. Which of the following sentences manages subjects and verbs most effectively?

   a. Currently, there is no defined career development process within headquarters.

   b. Currently, headquarters has no defined career development process.

   c. There is currently no defined career development process within headquarters.

   d. At the current time, there is no defined career development process within headquarters.

7. Which of the following sentences manages subjects and verbs most effectively?

   a. It is my hope that you will submit a proposal.

   b. I hope that you will submit a proposal.

   c. Your submission of a proposal is my hope.

   d. I hope that you will make a proposal submission.

8. Which of the following sentences manages subjects and verbs most effectively?

   a. The course will examine global supply and demand balances.

   b. The course will make an examination of global supply and demand balances.

   c. An examination of global supply and demand balances will be made by the course.

    d. There will be in the course an examination of global supply and demand balances.

9. Which of the following sentences manages subjects and verbs most effectively?

    a. The April meeting was canceled by action of the director.

    b. The cancellation of the April meeting was made by the director.

    c. The director declared the April meeting canceled.

    d. The director canceled the April meeting.

10. Which of the following sentences manages subjects and verbs most effectively?

    a. The writing process has five stages.

    b. There are five stages in the writing process.

    c. It is the case that the writing process has five stages.

    d. It is the case that there are five stages in the writing process.

Exercise B

Revise the following memo, managing subjects and verbs more effectively and making any other changes that will improve it.

There have been a number of public statements made by several of you about our company in recent weeks. These statements are believed by me to be harmful to the public image of the C&E Company.

    I made a referral of this matter to the Board of Directors, who held a discussion of it at some length. The Board made the decision that in the future all public statements about our company must be given advance clearance by this office. There are forms available for this purpose.

    Your cooperation in this matter will be appreciated.

MANAGE YOUR WRITING *TODAY*

On the very next writing job you have to do, begin with some writing management: Remind yourself that you're a writer, that writing can be managed, and that it's largely a matter of managing time. Set up blocks of time for planning, drafting, and revising—with more time allocated for planning and revising than for drafting.

- Then call in your Internal Editor to make the best possible "assignment" for this writing task. Begin by spending five minutes "finding the 'we.'" Take another five minutes to ask yourself, "What is the smallest community to which my audience and I both belong?" and "How are my audience and I alike and different in the four PACK dimensions: personality, attitude, circumstances, and knowledge?" Spend another five minutes to "make holes, not drills" by defining the purpose of the piece of writing.

Take another five minutes or so to "get your stuff together," to gather information for the piece of writing. Then end the planning stage with five minutes of "getting your ducks in a row," organizing your information to best achieve your purpose for your reader(s).

- Now "do it wrong the first time." Bring in your Internal Writer to draft your document, with as little interference as possible from your Internal Editor.

- Then take a break—for as long as you can, but for at least five minutes. Use this time to gain some objectivity about your draft and to "change hats" from your Internal Writer's rumpled fedora to your Internal Editor's eyeshade. When you return from the break, try to trick yourself into thinking that someone else wrote the draft, and look at it as if you're seeing it for the first time.

- Then revise your document using all the tools you already have in your toolbox. However, pay special attention to "signaling your turns," guiding your reader from sentence to sentence, and to "saying what you mean" by managing your subjects and verbs.

When you've finished, take a few minutes to evaluate how the process worked for you. Evaluate especially whether "saying what you mean" resulted in a more effective piece of writing at the end.

9

PAY BY THE WORD
MANAGE YOUR SENTENCE ECONOMY

ORMAN R. AUGUSTINE, president and chief executive officer (CEO) of Martin Marietta, once calculated the relationship between thickness and dollar amount of government contract proposals. After reporting the result, he wrote, "If all the proposals conforming to this standard were piled on top of each other at the bottom of the Grand Canyon, it would probably be a good idea."

Most readers of government and business writing agree that much of it is too long. But who's to blame? Pogo had the answer: "We have met the enemy, and he is us." Simply put, most of us in business and government use more words than we need to.

Some trainers and textbooks talk about conciseness or brevity. I prefer the word *economy* for two reasons. First, the words *conciseness* and *brevity* suggest that the best sentences are the shortest. But that's not always true. Remember when we added turn signals to a very "choppy" paragraph in Chapter 7? We actually made some sentences longer but also more effective. The word *economy,* however, suggests *value.* The most economical car is not necessarily the smallest or cheapest. It's the one that gives you the most of what you need at the lowest cost. Similarly, some sentences have to be relatively long to say what they mean. Economical sentences just don't use more words than they need.

The second reason I like the word *economy* is that it suggests money—euros, pounds, and dollars. Business is about money. As someone once said, in the game of business, money is how we keep score.

You see, many of us write as if we were getting paid by the word. This habit may come from our childhood and adolescence when we were assigned to write school papers with specific word counts: the famous 500-word theme, for example. In my early days as a teacher—before I knew better— I remember getting handwritten 500-word themes with a running word count in the margin—397, 440, 472, 489, 495—as the writer closed in on the magic number.

In fact, relatively few writers, and probably no business writers, get paid by the word. Instead, we pay by the word. Economic writing is writing that literally saves us money both in the short term and in the long term.

In the short term, writing costs money to produce, both in materials and in time. Norman Augustine, again, calculated that "a single copy of a winning proposal for a modern aircraft requires a document embodying a preparation cost per pound . . . about 400 times the cost per pound of the aircraft itself." One survey has estimated the total cost of the average business letter at about $100. This adds up.

What also adds up is the cost of failures to communicate, even to innovate, caused by unnecessarily wordy writing. Many companies are learning the value of sentence economy. A vice president at 3M, legendary for its innovation, told Tom Peters, "We consider a coherent sentence to be an acceptable first draft for a new-product plan."

But even more important, perhaps, is writing's long-term cost in terms of our readers' attention and goodwill. As Quentin E. Wood, CEO of Quaker State, once said, "When you say less, and say it more clearly, people remember more of it—and longer." This is so because, in fact, each unnecessary word costs us some of the attention and goodwill of each of our readers.

Consider this analogy. Suppose that next Monday you arrive at your office and find an envelope from me. Inside is a $10 bill. Tuesday and Wednesday you find the same. By Thursday, you're thinking about me during your commute, looking forward with pleasure to opening my envelope. By the time the last envelope comes on Friday, you're feeling very good about Ken Davis and the $50 I've sent you.

Now suppose, instead, that Monday's envelope holds a dollar. On Tuesday there's 25 cents, and on Wednesday there's 75 cents. You're intrigued but disappointed when Thursday's envelope, sealed with strapping tape, holds only a nickel. The letters keep coming, on into the next week and the weeks after, some with as much as a couple of dollars but most with small change. My envelopes become less and less important to you. Even if after several months you've received the same $50, you don't feel nearly as good about me. You've simply had to work too hard for the money.

This is how reading is. Reading a word is like opening an envelope: it requires a small but measurable amount of work. If each envelope or word contains something of value, we continue with anticipation. If most envelopes or words do not, we become bored and maybe give up. Thus, when you use 100 words instead of 200 to say something, you not only save money, but also have a much better chance of keeping your reader's attention and goodwill. In the early nineteenth century, British author C. C. Colton knew the secret of economy when he wrote, "That writer does the most who gives his reader the *most* knowledge, and takes from him the *least* time."

As you see in Figure 9-1, we're now at nine on the clock face, halfway through the revision stage of the writing process. Again, remember that revision tools are not rules, that you already have most of the revision tools you need, and most important, that revision tools are not drafting tools. To make your business writing more economical, do it as you revise, not as you draft. Don't interrupt the flow of that draft to worry about whether you've used too many words. Just put down the words as they come, even if you're going to cut some out later. American writer Truman Capote once said, "I believe more in the scissors than I do in the pencil."

OBJECTIVITY AND COMMON SENSE

Revising for economy is largely a matter of using two tools you already have: objectivity and common sense. After you've taken a break and returned to your draft as if you were reading it for the first time, you'll probably find

FIGURE 9-1   Pay by the word.

ways to cut words. Just read each sentence and ask yourself, "Do I need to say this? If so, do I need to use this many words?" Sometimes, like Rex's owner in Figure 9-2, you'll realize that what you first wrote isn't really true.

Look at this sentence:

The part is blue in color.

This is a sentence that any of us could have drafted. But at the revision stage you might realize that everyone knows that blue is a color. So revise the sentence to:

The part is blue.

The last two words of the original sentence added no meaning. They were already implied. Taking them off saves 33 percent; this is a savings any manager should be proud of.

Here's a similar sentence I've come across:

His mistakes were three (3) in number.

FIGURE 9-2 Rex the dog.

When I see this sentence, I'm tempted to say, "Not only does the writer not trust me to know that three is a number; he wants to make sure that I know which number it is." Seriously, this double numbering has its place, on checks and other documents that need to be errorproof and tamperproof, but there's absolutely no need for it in most business writing.

In his book, *Claw Your Way to the Top*, humorist Dave Barry provides a helpful question and answer: "Q. What do they mean on the TV weather forecast when they say we are going to have 'thundershower activity'? A. They mean we are not going to have an actual thunderstorm, per se, but we are going to have thundershower activity, which looks very similar to the untrained eye."

As you revise, be sure to let your common sense work both ways—not only for deciding to cut unnecessary words but also for deciding to keep necessary ones.

TWO TOOLS

Besides objectivity and common sense, two easy grammatical tools can help you to manage your sentence economy. The first is what William Strunk, Jr., and E. B. White, in their book, *Elements of Style*, call "which-hunting." To go on a "which-hunt," look for each use of the words *which, that*, and *who* (or a form of *who*) in your draft. (If you know school grammar, what you're looking for are relative clauses; if that term doesn't mean anything to you, just ignore this sentence.) Some uses of these words are necessary, but some can be eliminated by rearranging the sentence. For example, you can change the phrase "a commission that consists of 10 members" into "a 10-member commission." In doing so, you've gotten rid of three words, but more important, you've eliminated a whole clause your reader won't need to process. The reader will subconsciously thank you.

Similarly, you can revise this sentence:

The state has vast deposits of coal that have not yet been developed.

into this one:

The state has vast undeveloped coal deposits.

The other grammatical tool involves looking for prepositions: the little words such as *of, in, on, with,* and *for* that indicate the relationship between the noun that follows and something else in the sentence. In business writing, the most common preposition is probably *of*.

Like *which*'s, prepositions often are necessary, but they sometimes make a sentence uneconomical. For example, you can change

The fertilizer tablets are planted near the roots of the trees.

into:

The fertilizer tablets are planted near the tree roots.

And sometimes you'll hit a jackpot, as in this sentence:

The number of applications to schools of business is on the increase.

All four prepositions can be cut, leaving:

Business school applications are increasing.

BECKWITH ON ECONOMY

Recently, one of the strongest champions of economical writing has been best-selling marketing guru Harry Beckwith. In his book, *Selling the Invisible*, he wrote that vague, empty pieces of writing "tell your prospects one thing: They say you are willing to waste that person's time. No message can hurt you more." He continued, "Every prospect hopes you will heed the old New England proverb: 'Don't talk unless you can improve the silence.'"

And in his sequel, *The Invisible Touch*, Beckwith advised, "Skip the balderdash, the puffing, the filler: *Tell me*. Tell me the same way novelist Elmore Leonard (*Get Shorty*) writes books. Asked to explain why his books were so popular and so easy to read, Leonard answered: 'Simple. I just leave out the parts that readers skip.'"

EXERCISES

Exercise A

The following questions will test your understanding of this chapter. The final examination for this course will include similar questions.

1. Which of the following sentences is most economical without eliminating words that may carry important information?

   a. Textbook selection is accomplished through the use of a selection commission that consists of 10 members.

   b. Textbook selection is accomplished through the use of a 10-member selection commission.

   c. Textbooks are selected by a selection commission.

   d. Textbooks are selected by a 10-member commission.

2. Which of the following sentences is most economical without eliminating words that may carry important information?

   a. All unopened packages should be returned to the dock on 41st Street.

   b. All unopened packages should be returned to the 41st Street dock.

   c. All packages that are not opened should be returned to the dock on 41st Street.

   d. All packages that are not opened should be returned to the dock that is on 41st Street.

3. Which of the following sentences is most economical without eliminating words that may carry important information?

   a. Other factors that did not relate to an increased risk of cancer included . . .

   b. Other factors unrelated to an increased risk of cancer included . . .

   c. Other factors unrelated to an increased risk included . . .

   d. Other factors unrelated to an increased cancer risk included . . .

4. Which of the following sentences is most economical without eliminating words that may carry important information?

   a. The labels that are needed are rectangular in shape.

   b. The labels that are needed are rectangular.

   c. The needed labels are rectangular.

   d. The labels are rectangular.

5. Which of the following sentences is most economical without eliminating words that may carry important information?

   a. There are several projects that are successful which use volunteers.

   b. There are several successful projects that use volunteers.

   c. Several successful projects use volunteers.

   d. Several projects that are successful use volunteers.

6. Which of the following sentences is most economical without eliminating words that may carry important information?

   a. Please submit a report each week that lists all customer complaints.

   b. Please submit a report listing all customer complaints.

   c. Please submit a weekly report listing all customer complaints.

   d. Please submit a report each week listing all customer complaints.

7. Which of the following sentences is most economical without eliminating words that may carry important information?

   a. The agency will prepare a catalogue of the skills that each staff member possesses.

    b. The agency will catalogue each staff member's skills.

    c. The agency will prepare a catalogue of the skills of each staff member.

    d. The agency will prepare a catalogue of skills.

8. Which of the following sentences is most economical without eliminating words that may carry important information?

    a. The chairman will make a speech on the problems in marketing that the company has encountered.

    b. The chairman will speak on the problems in marketing that the company has encountered.

    c. The chairman will make a speech on the problems in marketing encountered by the company.

    d. The chairman will speak on the company's marketing problems.

9. Which of the following sentences is most economical without eliminating words that may carry important information?

    a. The costs of implementation will be offset by savings in time.

    b. The implementation costs will be offset by time savings.

    c. The costs of implementation will be offset by time savings.

    d. The implementation costs will be offset by savings in time.

10. Which of the following sentences is most economical without eliminating words that may carry important information?

    a. The process of writing has five (5) stages.

    b. The writing process has five (5) stages.

    c. The writing process has five stages.

    d. The process of writing has five stages.

Exercise B

Revise the following memo to make it more economical.

    I am writing to inform all of you of all the details of our new vacation policy, which will replace the old vacation policy.

    ■ Effective immediately, April 1, the anniversary of the birth of our founder, will be declared a company holiday. We are of the hope that the ultimate outcome of this extra day of released time will be an increase in the morale of the entire workforce.

    ■ We have arranged with a travel agency for them to provide vacation opportunities at reduced prices for company employees. They have a brochure that is available in the Personnel Office which gives a complete listing of all the tours that are to be offered.

- It is required that all managers submit reports of employee vacation preferences once each quarter.

Thank you. If you have any questions on this new policy, please feel free to call on me personally at your convenience at any time.

MANAGE YOUR WRITING *TODAY*

On the very next writing job you have to do, begin with some writing management: Remind yourself that you're a writer, that writing can be managed, and that it's largely a matter of managing time. Set up blocks of time for planning, drafting, and revising—with more time allocated for planning and revising than for drafting.

- Then call in your Internal Editor to make the best possible "assignment" for this writing task. Begin by spending five minutes "finding the 'we.'" Take another five minutes to ask yourself, "What is the smallest community to which my audience and I both belong?" and "How are my audience and I alike and different in the four PACK dimensions: personality, attitude, circumstances, and knowledge?" Spend another five minutes to "make holes, not drills" by defining the purpose of the piece of writing. Take another five minutes or so to "get your stuff together," to gather information for the piece of writing. Then end the planning stage with five minutes of "getting your ducks in a row," organizing your information to best achieve your purpose for your reader(s).

- Now "do it wrong the first time." Bring in your Internal Writer to draft your document with as little interference as possible from your Internal Editor.

- Then take a break—for as long as you can, but for at least five minutes. Use this time to gain some objectivity about your draft and to "change hats" from your Internal Writer's rumpled fedora to your Internal Editor's eyeshade. When you return from the break, try to trick yourself into thinking that someone else wrote the draft, and look at it as if you're seeing it for the first time.

- Then revise your document using all the tools you already have in your toolbox, as well as the tools you've learned so far in this course. Pay special attention to "paying by the word," making your sentences as economical as possible.

When you've finished, take a few minutes to evaluate how the process worked for you. Evaluate especially whether paying by the word resulted in a more effective piece of writing at the end.

Remember, you really are paying by the word. Make sure that each word is worth what it costs you.

10

TRANSLATE INTO ENGLISH
MANAGE YOUR WORD CHOICES

A S YOU SEE IN FIGURE 10-1, we're coming up toward 10 on our watch, so we're just past halfway through the revising stage of the writing process. In Chapter 7 we learned a tool for revising paragraphs, and in Chapters 8 and 9 we learned two sets of tools for revising sentences. In this chapter we'll learn a powerful tool for revising individual words—a tool to use in this five-minute segment of the writing process.

Remember that our job as business writers is not to use words that mean the right thing to *us*. Our job is to find the best words to convey our meaning to our reader(s). This is why the revision stage is so important. It frees us from having to settle on the first word that came to our mind at the drafting stage. It gives us a chance to choose, from a number of possible words, the one word that best gets the job done. As Mark Twain said, "The difference between the right word and the almost right word is the difference between lightning and the lightning-bug." To choose the right word, we need the right tools.

An especially powerful tool is one called "Translate into English." Naturally, this doesn't mean we need to translate from a foreign language. I mean that we need to translate from the kind of pseudo-English, "official" English, that all of us sometimes write. David Weinberger, in *The Cluetrain Manifesto* (perhaps the most important book on business communication in the last decade), calls such pseudo-English "The Standard Style." Weinberger writes, "Our business voice—in a managed environment—is virtually the

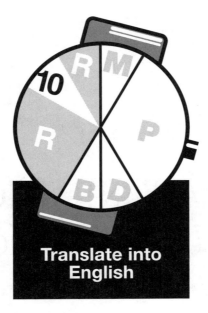

Translate into English

FIGURE 10-1   Translate into English.

same as everyone else's. . . . we learn to write memos in The Standard Style."
Unfortunately, this pseudo-English doesn't do that job very well.

Take this letter, for example. It's one my father received from a state
women's basketball governing body. He had asked them about running an
ad in their state tournament program.

Dear Mr. Davis:

Pursuant to your recent inquiry, please allow this communication to serve as
reply thereto.

The Girls' State Basketball Tournament wherein the souvenir program
is distributed commands an annual attendance of approximately 95,000 people. Additionally, we have a significant mailing to people in the middle west
who purchase the program in advance for use while either hearing the games
via radio or . . . .

And so it goes, for another page and a half.

Admittedly this is an extreme example of the kind of pseudo-English
I'm talking about. But it's not *that* extreme. I'm sure that it reminds you of
many letters, memos, e-mail messages, and reports that you've received—
or maybe even written.

This is an amazing fact about modern business. Some of the same people who like to think of themselves as on the cutting edge of technology, management theory, or marketing research still write the way people talked 200 years ago. They choose words that people haven't said to each other since they stopped wearing powdered wigs. When was the last time you heard a coworker say, "Pursuant to your recent inquiry"? Weinberger, again, writes: "We have been trained throughout our business careers to suppress our individual voice and to sound like a 'professional,' that is, to sound like everyone else. This professional voice is distinctive. And weird. Taken out of context, it is as mannered as the ritualistic dialogue of the seventeenth-century French court."

Yet language almost that old-fashioned appears every day in business writing. The late Malcolm Forbes called it as he saw it: "Business jargon too often is cold, stiff, unnatural. Suppose I came up to you and said, 'I acknowledge receipt of your letter, and I beg to thank you.' You'd think, 'Huh?'"

Don't get me wrong. In the right place and time, there's nothing wrong with elegance in language. But if our purpose is to get something done, to make something happen, then we need to make sure—at the revising stage of our writing—that we use the most effective words possible. As Joseph Pulitzer advised, "Put it before them briefly so they will read it, clearly so they will appreciate it, picturesquely so they will remember it and, above all, accurately so they will be guided by its light."

LEARNING FROM THE IRS

Here are two examples of writing from the U.S. Internal Revenue Service (IRS). The first is from the instruction book for the 1040 Income Tax Form for 1976. (After you read it, I'll tell you later why I went back that far for an example.)

1976
The Privacy Act of 1974 provides that each Federal Agency inform individuals, whom it asks to supply information, of the authority for the solicitation of the information and whether disclosure of such information is mandatory or voluntary; the principal purpose or purposes for which the information is to be used; the routine uses which may be made of the information; and the effects on the individual of not providing the requested information. This notification applies to the U.S. Individual Income Tax Returns, to declarations of estimated tax, to U.S. Gift Tax returns, and to any other tax return required to be filed by an individual and to schedules, statements, or other documents related to the returns, and any subsequent inquiries necessary to

complete, correct, and process the returns of taxpayers, to determine the correct tax liability and to collect any unpaid tax, interest, or penalty. . . .

The completion of all appropriate items requested by the return forms and related data is mandatory except for the Presidential Election Campaign Fund designation of the U.S. Individual Income Tax Returns, which is voluntary. . . .

Please retain this notification with your tax records and refer to it any time you are requested to furnish additional information.

In January 1977, just after the 1976 tax instructions were published, Jimmy Carter was sworn in as U.S. President. One of his first efforts from the White House was to make the language of government documents more effective. So in some areas of the government, some really quick revisions were cranked out that first year. By January 1978, when the 1977 tax instructions were published, they had been greatly revised. Here's the same passage one year later:

1977
The Privacy Act of 1974 says that each Federal agency that asks for information must tell you the following:
    1. Its legal right to ask for the information and whether the law says you must give it.
    2. What purpose the agency has in asking for it, and the use to which it will be put.
    3. What could happen if you do not give it.
For the Internal Revenue Service the law covers the following:
    1. Tax returns and any papers you file with them.
    2. Any questions we need to ask you so we can
        (a) complete, correct, or process your returns,
        (b) figure your tax, and
        (c) collect tax, interest or penalties. . . .
You must fill in all parts of the tax form that apply to you. But you do not have to check the boxes for the Presidential Election Campaign Fund. You can skip it if you wish. . . .

Please keep this notice with your records. It may help you if we ask you for other information.

These two samples say exactly the same thing. By law, they have to. We can be sure that before the 1977 revision was published, a whole troop of IRS lawyers signed off on it. But even though these versions say the same thing, the 1977 version is much, much easier to read and understand.

What kinds of improvements did the IRS make? Perhaps the most obvious is turning long sentences into outlines and lists. This is almost always a good idea. In the memos, letters, and reports we write, we should always look for ways to use numbered or bulleted lists instead of long sentences or paragraphs.

A second improvement is the use of "turn signals," the tool we learned in Chapter 7. Both the colon in the first sentence and the *but* near the end make the document easier to follow.

Another improvement is in the choice of subjects and verbs, the topic of Chapter 8. In one sentence, the subject and verb combination "completion is (mandatory)" was changed to "you must fill in." And still another improvement is economy, as discussed in Chapter 9. The 1977 version is about 13 percent shorter.

The most important improvement, however, may be less obvious. It occurs in individual words. More than a dozen words were replaced by simpler synonyms:

1976	1977
provides	says
inform	tell
individuals	you
authority	right
solicit	ask
provide	give
effects	what could happen
inquire	ask
complete	fill in
voluntary	you can skip
retain	keep
request	ask
additional	other

WORD HISTORIES

To understand the difference between the 1976 and 1977 lists, it may help to go back in history. (If you're not a history buff, feel free to skim this section.) The English language really began in the fifth century A.D. when tribes from what is now Denmark and northern Germany invaded Britain, pushing the native Celts back into Scotland, Ireland, and Wales. One of these tribes, the Angles, gave their name to the new country—Angle-land, or England—and to its language, which we now call Old English. When we look at something written in Old English (like the great epic poem *Beowulf,* for example), it looks more like German than like modern English. And Germany, of course, is where it came from.

This Germanic language soon became widely used for government and business, as well as for everyday life. It lasted as the principal language of England until 1066, when a French Duke, William of Normandy, crossed the Channel with a French army and defeated the English army near a town called Hastings. William's victorious army marched into London, and on

Christmas Day 1066, Duke William was crowned King William, William I of England. He became known as William the Conqueror.

William and his conquering forces spoke a Latinate language, an early form of French. So as he set up a new government over the conquered English, he imposed a new language on the country, as Figure 10-2 illustrates. For the next couple of centuries, both languages existed in England: French as the official language of government and business and English as the everyday language of most common people.

Gradually, the languages merged into what we now call Middle English. This language kept the structure and basic vocabulary of Old English but included a great number of French-origin words. Then, just as this merger was becoming complete, a new invasion came—not military this time but cultural. The Renaissance was spreading northward and westward from the Mediterranean. With its rebirth of learning and culture, it brought thousands of new French and Italian words. As a result of these two invasions—the military invasion of William the Conqueror and the cultural invasion of the Renaissance—English ended up with more words than any other language in the world.

In activities such as farming that were untouched by either invasion, today's English words are largely Old English in origin. We often can recognize them as shorter and simpler. However, in certain activities, such as

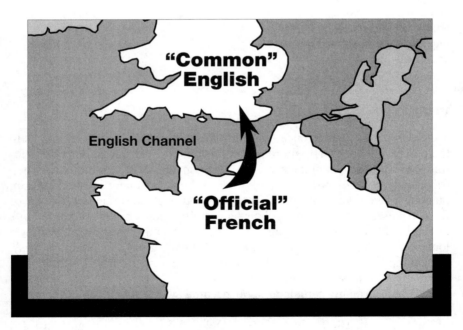

FIGURE 10-2   The Norman Conquest.

the performing arts, which had their rebirth in the Latin countries, our words are largely French or Italian in origin. They are often longer words. John Brunner, in his science fiction novel, *The Shockwave Rider*, demonstrates this difference:

> This is a basic place, a farm. Listen to it.

> Land. House. Barn. Sun. Rain. Snow. Field. Fence. Pond. Corn. Wheat. Hay. Plow. Sow. Reap. Horse. Pig. Cow.

> This is an abstract place, a concert hall. Listen to it.

> Conductor. Orchestra. Audience. Overture. Concerto. Symphony. Podium. Harmony. Instrument. Oratorio. Variations. Arrangement. Violin, Clarinet. Piccolo. Tympani. Pianoforte. Auditorium.

As Brunner points out, you can "listen" to the difference between the two sets of words. The words in the "farm" list sound plainer; the words in the "concert hall" list sound fancier. Those in the first list are of Germanic origin: Forms of these words were used by English farmers before and after the Norman Conquest. Those in the second list are from French and Latin, brought in, as needed, to a society that had no native words for the stuff of concert halls.

A related pair of lists compares the words we use for kinds of meat and the animals they come from:

beef	cow
pork	pig, swine
mutton	sheep
venison	deer

In the years after the Norman Conquest, the people down at the barn taking care of the animals spoke Old English—so we get our animal names from them. The people around the table at the castle eating the good cuts of meat spoke French—so we get our meat names from them.

Many concepts, of course, were part of the language of both Old English and Norman French speakers. These include many common nouns, adjectives, adverbs, and (especially) verbs. As a result, Modern English has a very large number of synonyms from French/Latin and English/German sources. Here are some examples:

French/Latin	English/German
converse	talk
frequently	often
proceed	go
require	need

initial	first
dispatch	send
depart	leave
discover	find

An amazing fact, when you think about it, is that now, more than 900 years after the Norman Conquest, these two lists of words still carry a class difference. The French/Latin words still seem to us fancier and more "educated," just as the French-speaking officials must have seemed in the eleventh and twelfth centuries. The English/German words still seem to us plainer and less "educated," just as the Old English–speaking peasants must have seemed then.

As a result, the French/Latin words tend to find their way into "official" writing—the writing done in business, government, and the professions. Perhaps a desire to sound "official" caused the writer of the 1976 tax instructions to use so many French/Latin words. In fact, the 1976 word list above is made up entirely of French/Latin words.

This wouldn't be a problem except for one important fact: writing made up heavily of Latinate words is more difficult to read. The longer Latinate words slow down reading and lead to less understanding, even for well-educated readers. Germanic-origin words, on the other hand, make writing more readable. Even educated readers find these shorter, plainer words generally more effective. The revised 1977 list is made up entirely of words of Germanic origin.

The reason for the difference in readability does not lie so much in the history of our language as in the personal history of each individual reader. The English/German words are, in most cases, the ones we all learn first as children. The words in the right-hand lists above are probably among the first thousand words an English-speaking child learns. When the child grows to adulthood, he continues to use these words most. One authority claims that of the 100 most commonly used words in our language all are of English/German origin. Thus it's no wonder that a passage such as the 1977 tax instructions made up of these simpler words will be read more easily and will communicate its content more effectively.

At this point you may be thinking, "Sure, you have to use simpler words in tax instructions because they have to be read by people with all levels of education, including grade-school dropouts. But if you're writing to someone with a lot more education, you should use bigger words."

Wrong. Even people with graduate and professional degrees will find the 1977 tax instructions easier to read than the 1976 instructions. No matter how much schooling we eventually get, the Germanic words remain more familiar, more easily accessible to our reading minds.

So a powerful tool for revising the words in your business writing is this: Unless you have a good reason otherwise, substitute plainer

(English/German) words for fancier (French/Latin) words. In other words, "Translate into English."

You'll make your readers very happy. As "Rosa's Buzz-off Theory" (quoted in Paul Dickson's *The Official Rules*) states, "After completing that memo or report, substitute each buzz word with an everyday word. All on distribution will feel self-congratulatory at having for once understood a piece of writing in total. You will make friends."

The result also can have a direct payoff for your business. In his now-classic book on service marketing, *Selling the Invisible,* marketing guru Harry Beckwith writes, "The famous direct-mail writer John Caples once changed one word in an ad—substituting 'fix' for 'repair'—and increased the response to the ad 20 percent." By now you should be able to recognize that the exact tool that Caples used was "Translate into English."

To use this tool, you certainly don't need to know German and French. You don't even need to look up word origins in a dictionary—although it sometimes can be interesting and fun to do so. (The *American Heritage Dictionary* is especially good for word origins.) All you have to do is sub-stitute words that a child can understand, and your writing will be more readable, and more effective, for adult readers as well. As Fergus O'Connell writes in *The Competitive Advantage of Common Sense*, "The key to being good at marketing is to be able to explain—very simply—why someone should buy what you sell. If you can tell it to me like I'm a six-year-old, then you will be a great marketer."

GOOD REASONS OTHERWISE

You may have noticed that the tool carries the qualification "unless you have a good reason otherwise." One reason is *precision*. Many fancier Latinate words are necessary for their precise meaning. And as Albert Einstein once said, "Things should be made as simple as possible—but no simpler." The "concert hall" list showed that there are plenty of meanings for which no simple Germanic words exist. The Latinate word *manufacture*, for example, once meant the same thing as the Germanic word *make*, but over the years, *manufacture* has taken on connotations of large-scale, mechanized "mak-ing" that give it a place of its own in our language. I *make* cookies; Keebler *manufactures* them. I *make* hamburgers; McDonald's *manufactures* them.

Sometimes, too, you will want to choose a fancier word for *variety*. If you have used *get* several times in a passage, you may want to substitute *obtain, secure,* or *acquire* sometimes. (This is why you may once have been taught to use longer words. At lower grade levels, it's important to expand our vocabulary.)

Finally, you may want to choose a Latinate word for reasons of *cour-tesy* (a Latinate word itself, derived from the word for the king's court). You sometimes may find it more polite, for example, to *inform* people than to *tell* them.

Naturally, you may be concerned that using simpler words will make you seem less educated or less intelligent. But the great speakers and writers always have known that they are communicating to express, not impress. Ultimately, you must impress your reader or listener with your ideas, not your vocabulary, and a simple, direct vocabulary will help you to get those ideas across more effectively. Malcolm Forbes said it well: "Pretense invariably impresses only the pretender."

One of the great leaders—and great communicators—of the past century was British Prime Minister Winston Churchill. His speeches and writing gave courage to his nation during its most perilous time. But as someone once observed, think how ineffective Churchill would have been during World War II if he had said, "I have nothing to offer except hemoglobin, physical exertion, lachrymal secretions, and perspiration." No, what he said in his first statement as prime minister, on May 13, 1940, was, "I have nothing to offer except blood, toil, tears, and sweat." Churchill shared his secret when he wrote, in a sentence made up entirely of one-syllable, English-origin words, "Short words are best and the old words when short are best of all."

Churchill's friend and ally, Franklin D. Roosevelt, also was a master of "translating into English." According to Edward T. Thompson, former editor-in-chief of *Reader's Digest,* "A speech writer for President Franklin D. Roosevelt wrote, 'We are endeavoring to construct a more inclusive society.' FDR changed it to, 'We're going to make a country in which no one is left out.'"

You also may have to overcome an organizational culture that favors difficult language. But make sure that you know what the expectations, in fact, are. My friend Kitty O. Locker, in her book, *Business and Administrative Communication,* writes: "If you think your boss doesn't want you to write simply, ask him or her. A few bosses do prize flowery language. Most don't."

Admittedly, some prejudices have to be overcome. William K. Zinsser, in his wonderful book, *On Writing Well,* says: "Executives at every level are prisoners of the notion that a simple style reflects a simple mind. Actually, a simple style is the result of hard work and hard thinking; a muddy style reflects a muddy thinker or a person too lazy to organize his thoughts." And Patricia T. O'Conner and Stewart Kellerman, in their book, *You Send Me,* note that "Some puffed-up writers use long words, techie talk, trendy terms, and convoluted sentences to cover up or deceive or sound important or go along with the crowd. Most people who inflate their writing, though, are simply insecure, often for no good reason. They don't feel their ideas are strong enough, and they prop them up with elaborate language."

They continue: "If your ideas are any good, they can stand on their own. So kick away those unnecessary props. All they do is turn a strong writer into a wuss."

One of former Chrysler Chairman Lee Iacocca's "Eight Command-
ments of Good Management" is "Say it in English and keep it short."
Chapter 9 gave tools for honoring the second part of Iacocca's commandment. In this chapter you've learned a powerful tool for honoring the first
part: "Say it in English."

SEC GUIDELINES

The U.S. Securities and Exchange Commission (SEC) has done a wonderful job of "maximizing" (to use cartoonist Jerry Van Amerongen's
buzzword in Figure 10-3) the use of plain language in documents within
SEC control.

In its guidelines, the SEC makes direct use of the tool we've been calling "Translate into English." SEC guidelines advise, "Surround complex
ideas with short, common words. For example, use *end* instead of *termi-
nate*, *explain* rather than *elucidate*, and *use* instead of *utilize*. When a shorter, simpler synonym exists, use it."

As an example, the SEC recommends changing this sentence:

FIGURE 10-3   The buzzword, management-style.

Sandyhill Basic Value Fund, Inc. (the "Fund") seeks *capital appreciation* and, secondarily, income by investing in securities, primarily equities, that management of the Fund believes are *undervalued* and therefore represent *basic investment value.*

into this sentence:

At the Sandyhill Basic Value Fund, we will strive to increase the value of your shares (capital appreciation) and, to a lesser extent, to provide income (dividends). We will invest primarily in undervalued stocks, meaning those selling for low prices given the financial strength of the companies.

Similarly, the SEC recommends revising:

No *consideration* or *surrender* of Beco Stock will be required of shareholders of Beco in return for the shares of Unis Common Stock *issued pursuant to the Distribution.*

into:

You will not have to turn in your shares of Beco stock or pay any money to receive your shares of Unis common stock from the spin-off.

Finally, the "before" and "after" SEC examples in Figures 10-4 and 10-5 sum up much of what we've learned in Chapters 7 through 10.

READABILITY FORMULAS AND STYLE CHECKERS

A number of "readability formulas," both manual and computer-based, have been developed to measure the difficulty of written work. Perhaps the most widely used is part of the "grammar checker" built into Microsoft Word. It and some others claim to report the number of years of schooling required to read a document.

However, in the words of the SEC,

You should be aware of a major flaw in every readability formula. No formula takes into account the content of the document being evaluated. In other words, no formula can tell you if you have conveyed the information clearly. For the most part, they count the numbers of syllables and words in a sentence and the number of sentences in the sample. Of course, if you applied a readability formula to a traditional disclosure document, it would fail miser-

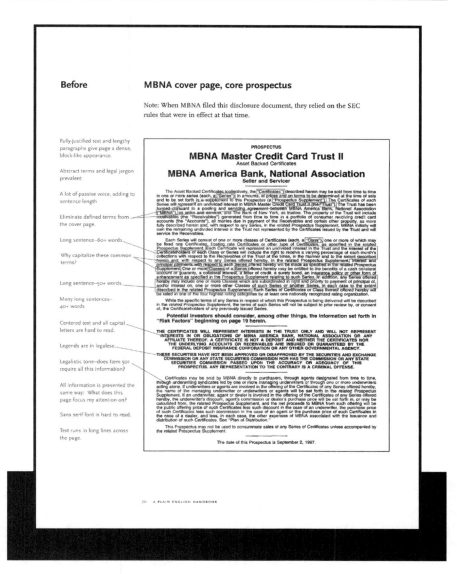

FIGURE 10-4   SEC "before" document.

ably. But keep in mind that by some formulas' calculations, Einstein's theory of relativity reads at a 5th grade level.

The SEC continues:

Some computerized style checkers analyze your grammar and identify the passive voice. They may suggest ways to make your writing more "readable."

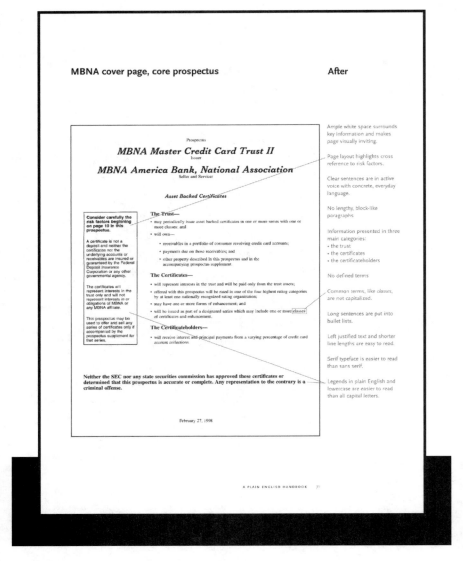

FIGURE 10-5   SEC "after" document.

Take their suggestions as just that—suggestions. The final test of whether any piece of writing meets its goal of communicating information comes when humans read it.

If you would like some "numbers" on the readability of a draft, here's a simple tool you can use—a tool that takes an actual reader into account.

This tool is based on the fact that at the level of sentences and words, the most readable writing is also the most predictable. Readable writing generally (not always, of course) fulfills the reader's expectations. Therefore, you can test the readability of a draft by obliterating selected words and having a reader guess what they are. To run such a test:

1. Count back 50, 100, or 200 words from the end of your draft. (The exact number doesn't matter.)
2. Go through this ending and replace every fifth or every tenth word with a blank. Make all blanks the same length, regardless of the length of the words they replace.
3. Save this changed draft under a different name (so that you can get back to your original).
4. Have someone else read this copy of your draft and guess the missing words.
5. Note the "hits" and "misses," and decide whether each "miss" could have been a "hit" if it or words before it were changed. (Not all "misses" are bad things. Any writing will, and should, have some surprises.)
6. If you discover areas where rewriting is needed, do similar rewriting throughout your draft.

DELIBERATE "OBFUSCATION"?

Because fancy words can keep communication from happening, they can be used when you really don't want your message to be read and understood. One example may be the following recall notice from a car company that will remain anonymous:

> A defect which involves the possible failure of a frame support plate may exist on your vehicle. This plate (front suspension pivot bar support plate) connects a portion of the front suspension to the vehicle frame, and its failure could affect vehicle directional control, particularly during heavy brake application. In addition, your vehicle may require adjustment to the hood secondary catch system. The secondary catch may be misaligned so that the hood may not be adequately restrained to prevent hood fly-up in the event the primary catch is inadvertently left unengaged. Sudden hood fly-up beyond the secondary catch while driving could impair driver visibility. In certain circumstances, occurrence of either of the above conditions could result in vehicle crash without prior warning.

A cynic might read this notice and observe that the manufacturer complied with the law by sending this document but didn't really want many people to bring in their cars for repair.

Here's another real-life example that I suspect is deliberate—though not for a dishonest purpose. Rather, I suspect that a bored, low-level soldier or civilian at the Department of Defense (DOD) decided to test how far he or she could push DOD jargon:

2.1.1 Specifications and standards
Unless otherwise specified, the following specifications and standards of the issue listed in that issue of the Department of Defense Index of Specifications and Standards (DoDISS) specified in the solicitation, form a part of this specification to the extent specified herein.

Humorists have had a field day with this kind of language. Robert Thornton suggests, in his book, *Lexicon of Intentionally Ambiguous Recommendations* (*LIAR*, for short), that when we write recommendation letters, we actually might *want* to use confusing language. Among his examples are:

"You'll be lucky to get him to work for you."
"He doesn't mind being disturbed."
"He's a man of many convictions."
"You simply won't believe this woman's credentials."
"I most enthusiastically recommend this man with no qualifications whatsoever."

Dave Barry, in *Claw Your Way to the Top*, advises, "Use the word 'transpire' a lot. Wrong: The dog barked. Right: What transpired was, the dog barked. Even better: A barking of the dog transpired."

Mike Shor has developed a Web-based tool called "MBA-Writer" for automatically generating "sentences ready for inclusion into your business memos without all of the thinking." Here are the first three sentences it generated for me:

- Realigning core competencies, the asynchronous transitional capability internalizes an enterprise-wide value framework.
- Within an impactful environment, leveraging customer positions collaboratively and interdependently disseminates the shifting of age-old paradigms.
- In layman's terms, our contingency schematic requires further offline considerations of multiproduct decisioning.

And *Dilbert*'s creator, Scott Adams, writes, "If you want to advance in management, you have to convince other people that you're smart. This is accomplished by substituting incomprehensible jargon for common words. For example, a manager would never say, 'I used my fork to eat a potato.'

A manager would say, 'I utilized a multitined tool to process a starch resource.' The two sentences mean almost the same thing, but the second one is obviously from a smarter person."

Seriously, you have to make the ethical decision about which way to use this tool. You can use it to change plain words to fancy ones in order to hide their meaning. However, if you truly want to get your message across, "Translate into English."

THREE EXAMPLES

Before we get to the exercises for this chapter, I want to show you three examples of simple, powerful business writing, all taken from *The Forbes Book of Great Business Letters*. First is an 1848 letter (in its entirety) from business giant Cornelius Vanderbilt to his former agents:

> You have undertaken to cheat me. I won't sue you, for the law is too slow. I'll ruin you.

The second is from a memo from Roger Enrico, president and CEO of Pepsi-Cola USA, to all bottlers and employees. The year was 1985. The occasion was rival Coca-Cola's introduction of New Coke:

> There is no question the long-term market success of Pepsi has forced this move. Everyone knows when something is right it doesn't need changing. Maybe they finally realized what most of us have known for years . . . Pepsi tastes better than Coke.

The third is from a message from Tom Paquin, manager at Netscape, encouraging engineers to meet a release deadline:

> We do whatever it takes. And feel damn great about it when we pull it off.

As sports agent Mark H. McCormack wrote, "Short words, short sentences, short paragraphs work. Trust me."

EXERCISES

Exercise A

The following questions will test your understanding of this chapter. The final examination for this course will include similar questions.

1. Which of the following sentences uses words most effectively?

a. The report is intended to provide information on a monthly basis to senior management and others as necessary.

b. The report is meant to provide monthly information to senior management and others as necessary.

c. The report is intended to provide information on a monthly basis to senior management and needed others.

d. The report will get monthly information to senior managers and others.

2. Which of the following sentences uses words most effectively?

a. As we examine our position in relation to supporting the fund drive, it seems that we will be unable to participate at the same level we did in 2004.

b. We won't be able to give as much to the fund drive as we did in 2004.

c. As we examine our position in relation to supporting the fund drive, it seems that we will be unable to contribute at the same level we did in 2004.

d. As we review our position in relation to supporting the fund drive, it appears that we will be unable to participate at the same level we did in 2004.

3. Which of the following sentences uses words most effectively?

a. The above information provides necessary information in evaluating the extent of opportunity available.

b. The above information provides information necessary for the evaluation of the extent of opportunity available.

c. This information tells us what we need to make a decision.

d. This information is necessary for evaluating the extent of opportunity available.

4. Which of the following sentences uses words most effectively?

a. After reviewing the data, we will talk with you about what happens next.

b. After reviewing the data, we will be in contact with you to determine next steps as warranted.

c. After reviewing the data, we will be in contact with you to determine next steps.

d. After reviewing the data, we will contact you to determine next steps as warranted.

5. Which of the following sentences uses words most effectively?

a. We did not attempt to estimate the potential negative effect on our business.

b. We did not attempt to estimate the potential negative impact on our business.

c. We did not attempt to calculate the potential negative effect on our business.

d. We did not try to estimate the potential harm to our business.

6. Which of the following sentences uses words most effectively?

   a. If you agree, please contact the Foundation and advise them that you are our company's representative and that all future correspondence should be directed to you.

   b. If you agree, please tell the Foundation that you are our representative and ask them to send all mail to you.

   c. If you agree, please contact the Foundation and tell them that you are our company's representative and that all future correspondence should be sent to you.

   d. If you agree, please contact the Foundation and tell them that you are our company's representative and request that they direct all future correspondence to you.

7. Which of the following sentences uses words most effectively?

   a. I would like for you to investigate the feasibility of managing the timely clearance of priority items from your area.

   b. I would like for you to look into the feasibility of managing the timely clearance of priority items from your area.

   c. Please investigate the feasibility of managing the timely clearance of priority items from your area.

   d. Please look into how you can clear priority items on time.

8. Which of the following sentences uses words most effectively?

   a. The chairman will present a speech on the difficulties in marketing that the company has encountered.

   b. The chairman will speak on the difficulties in marketing that the company has encountered.

   c. The chairman will make a speech on the problems in marketing encountered by the company.

   d. The chairman will speak on the company's marketing problems.

9. Which of the following sentences uses words most effectively?

   a. The Girls' State Basketball Tournament wherein the souvenir program is distributed commands an annual attendance of approximately 95,000 people.

   b. The Girls' State Basketball Tournament, where the souvenir program is distributed, draws about 95,000 people each year.

   c. The Girls' State Basketball Tournament wherein the souvenir program is distributed draws an attendance of approximately 95,000 people annually.

   d. The Girls' State Basketball Tournament, where the souvenir program is distributed, commands an annual attendance of about 95,000 people.

10. Which of the following sentences uses words most effectively?

    a. The process of written composition possesses five successive stages.

    b. The process of written composition has five stages.

    c. The writing process has five stages.

    d. The process of written composition possesses five stages.

Exercise B

Revise the following memo to make it more economical.

> As I've conversed with many of you over the past several months, I've frequently heard you inquire, "Are we attempting to manufacture too many new products? Do we really require such an extensive line?"
>
> My initial response is to emphasize the importance of altering our company's image. To obtain our share of the market, we must rectify the faults of the past. We must be perceived as a company willing to institute innovations and progress into new areas.
>
> I'm confident that if you scrutinize the matter, you will discover that I am correct.

MANAGE YOUR WRITING *TODAY*

On the very next writing job you have to do, begin with some writing management: Remind yourself that you're a writer, that writing can be managed, and that it's largely a matter of managing time. Set up blocks of time for planning, drafting, and revising—with more time allocated for planning and revising than for drafting.

- Then call in your Internal Editor to make the best possible "assignment" for this writing task. Begin by spending five minutes "finding the 'we.'" Take another five minutes to ask yourself, "What is the smallest community to which my audience and I both belong?" and "How are my audience and I alike and different in the four PACK dimensions: personality, attitude, circumstances, and knowledge?" Spend another five minutes to "make holes, not drills" by defining the purpose of the piece of writing. Take another five minutes or so to "get your stuff together," to gather information for the piece of writing. Then end the planning stage with five minutes of "getting your ducks in a row," organizing your information to best achieve your purpose for your reader(s).

- Now "do it wrong the first time." Bring in your Internal Writer to draft your document with as little interference as possible from your Internal Editor.

- Then take a break—for as long as you can, but for at least five minutes. Use this time to gain some objectivity about your draft and to "change hats" from your Internal Writer's rumpled fedora to your Internal Editor's eyeshade.

- When you return from the break, try to trick yourself into thinking that someone else wrote the draft, and look at it as if you're seeing it for the first time. Then revise your document using all the tools you already have in your toolbox, as well as the tools you've learned so far in this book. Pay special attention to "translating into English," making your words as simple as possible—but, as Einstein said—not more so.

When you've finished, take a few minutes to evaluate how the process worked for you. Evaluate especially whether translating into English resulted in a more effective piece of writing at the end.

11

FINISH THE JOB
MANAGE YOUR SPELLING,
PUNCTUATION, AND MECHANICS

WHAT ARE YOUR BIGGEST communication problems? When I asked this question to several hundred businesspeople, their number one answer was "speaking to a group," followed by "being persuasive in my speaking and writing." But high on the list—in fact, the highest problem on the list specific to writing —was "using correct spelling and punctuation."

I call this "finishing the job." I've chosen the phrase carefully to take advantage of the two ways we use the verb *finish:* to mean "end" (as in "I've finished the work") and to mean "put a surface on" (as in "I've finished this table with varnish").

The first meaning of *finish* is important for our purpose because, as shown in Figure 11-1, spelling and punctuation should be the *end* of our writing process, the last thing we think about before sending the letter, memo, or report to our reader(s). Most of us worry about spelling and punctuation much too early in the writing process. As a result, several bad things happen:

- We interrupt the flow of our drafting.
- We waste time correcting words and sentences we might later decide not to use at all.
- We commit ourselves to the concept of perfection too early, thus blinding ourselves to changes that really might need to be made.

Finish the Job

FIGURE 11-1   Finish the job.

So we need to remind ourselves that spelling and punctuation are the way in which we *finish* the process.

The second meaning of *finish* is important for our purpose because spelling and punctuation are nothing more or less than the *finish,* or surface, on a piece of writing. On one hand, this makes them very important: They're the first thing our reader sees and judges us on. As Mark H. McCormack wrote in *What They* Still *Don't Teach You at Harvard Business School,* "Only sloppy executives send out sloppy memos. Perfect grammar and perfect proofreading display professionalism and courtesy to the reader. Even if your suggestions are shot down, you will earn credibility." The late Malcolm Forbes said it too: "Make it perfect. No typos, no misspellings, no factual errors. If you're sloppy and let mistakes slip by, the person reading your letter will think you don't know better or don't care. Do you?"

On the other hand, the fact that spelling and punctuation are just *finish* keeps their importance in perspective. Just as a shiny coat of paint can't make up for a badly engineered or badly built car underneath, so a perfect spelling and punctuation job can't make up for a badly conceived or written letter.

One reason most Americans (including me) think of ourselves as poor spellers may be a frustration at those endless spelling tests we all took in school. But there's a more important reason for our insecurity—and it's not our fault. We English speakers have inherited what is almost surely the world's most difficult language to spell.

Speakers of Spanish, Russian, or Japanese have much less trouble with spelling. Their languages have developed more straightforwardly, with a neater fit between spelling and pronunciation. English, however, doesn't have such a neat fit, and so it *causes* fits. English developed in twists and turns, absorbing elements from various other languages at various times. Moreover, it developed the idea of consistent spelling late. A seventeenth-century merchant might even have spelled his own name differently from one day to the next. Even Shakespeare seems to have done so.

Thus English has become a nightmare of spelling quirks. Imagine someone trying to learn our language. She is told that the word *cough* is pronounced "coff"; *tough*, however, is not "toff," but "tuff." Add an *h* to make it *though,* and you get "thoff"? No. "thuff"? No. "thoe"! And inserting an *r* to make it *through* gives you a fourth sound, "threw."

We native speakers usually don't have trouble with these words. Our problem is not with spellings that produce multiple sounds but with sounds that have multiple or unusual spellings. Our problems are with *ie* and *ei*, with *ance* and *ence*, and with single and double consonants. No wonder we are bad spellers.

Yet, for a people who *are* bad spellers, we Americans are not especially forgiving of bad spelling by each other. We businesspeople in particular single out spelling more than anything else when getting a first impression of a piece of writing. Two or three misspelled words in an otherwise brilliant job application letter can doom that letter to the wastebasket faster than anything else. Reporter Bob Considine has framed what he calls "Considine's Law": "Whenever one word or letter can change the entire meaning of a sentence, the probability of an error being made will be in direct proportion to the embarrassment it will cause."

So what's the answer? Here are several:

- *When you write with a computer, use a spell-checker.* Most word processing programs now come with built-in dictionaries, and they can save you a lot of time and embarrassment. Remember, though, to spell-check only *after* you have written a draft, not *while* you are drafting. Interrupting a draft to worry about spelling can take your attention away from more important concerns (so turn off that on-the-fly spell-checker in Microsoft Word). Remember, too, that spell-checkers don't relieve you of the responsibility of improving your spelling skills. For one thing, they can't catch all errors, especially errors that result in real words with different meanings, such as *there* and *three*. For another, most of us still do lots of writing without a computer: forms, handwritten messages, and the like.
- *Proofread carefully.* Use the professional proofreader's trick of reading your writing backwards, a word at a time. Starting from

the end and reading to the beginning forces you to see each word *as a word*, not as part of a larger meaning. And of course, whenever possible, ask someone else to proofread for you; you can return the favor.

- *When in doubt, look it up.* Keep a good dictionary on your desk, and use it often. (Be sure to get a reputable, up-to-date dictionary. See Appendix D for recommendations.)
- *Track your spelling problems.* When you look up a word, put a tick mark beside it in your dictionary. Do the same when your spell-checker finds a mistake. You'll build your own inventory of words you need to learn.
- *Consider learning three or four spelling rules.* If your problems are with *ie* and *ei* or with what to do with *y*, silent *e*, or single consonants when adding suffixes, there are rules that can help. You can get them from many handbooks.
- *Make up your own tricks.* When a word repeatedly gives you trouble, make up the silliest, most juvenile trick you can for it. As a teacher and trainer, I often have to write the word *attendance*, but I could never remember whether it ended with *ance* or *ence* until someone told me to remember "Attendance at a dance." So now that's what goes through my mind every time I write the word. Don't laugh—the trick saves me from looking it up.

These tips won't make you a perfect speller. Given the nature of our language, few people ever spell it perfectly. With a little effort, though, you can reduce your errors considerably.

The bad news about punctuation is that it is even less standardized than spelling. Each English-speaking country, each profession, each publication, and even each company seems to have its own official or unofficial rules about what and how to punctuate when. The best advice about this diversity of rules, therefore, is to find out if the company or publication you're writing for has an official style sheet, and stick to it.

The *good* news about punctuation is that there is much less to learn about it than about spelling. English has hundreds of thousands of words but fewer than a dozen commonly used punctuation marks. So begin paying attention to them and turning to a handbook when you need help. Soon you'll be competing confidently with Graham in the Emphatic Punctuation Contest (Figure 11-2).

Together, a few punctuation rules and the spelling tips listed earlier may give you more skill and confidence as a writer. They can't turn bad writing into good, but they may help you put those important finishing touches on an already good document.

FIGURE 11-2   Graham is an easy winner in the "period" category.

EXERCISE

The final examination for this course will include questions similar to the following. As you answer these questions, remember that they're diagnostic, designed to include some of the most common spelling and punctuation problems. Pay attention to the correct answers to the questions you miss. They will tell you what you especially need to work on.

1. Which of the following sentences is most conventional in spelling, punctuation, and mechanics?

   a. Please return the voltmeter to its case.

   b. Please return the voltmeter to it's case.

   c. Please return the voltmeter to its' case.

   d. None of these answers uses conventional spelling.

2. Which of the following sentences is most conventional in spelling, punctuation, and mechanics?

   a. In his letter to us, he said that our proposal was alot of "hot air".

   b. In his letter to us, he said that our proposal was a lot of "hot air".

   c. In his letter to us, he said that our proposal was alot of "hot air."

   d. In his letter to us, he said that our proposal was a lot of "hot air."

3. Which of the following sentences is most conventional in spelling, punctuation, and mechanics?

   a. When will the new stationary be printed?

   b. When will the new stationery be printed?

   c. When will the new stationary be printted?

   d. When will the new stationery be printted?

4. Which of the following sentences is most conventional in spelling, punctuation, and mechanics?

   a. The new tax law will effect our accounting system; it also will have a major affect on our tax flow.

   b. The new tax law will effect our accounting system; it also will have a major effect on our tax flow.

   c. The new tax law will affect our accounting system; it also will have a major affect on our tax flow.

   d. The new tax law will affect our accounting system; it also will have a major effect on our tax flow.

5. Which of the following sentences is most conventional in spelling, punctuation, and mechanics?

   a. Abu Dhabi is the capitol and principle city of the United Arab Emirates.

   b. Abu Dhabi is the capitol and principal city of the United Arab Emirates.

   c. Abu Dhabi is the capital and principle city of the United Arab Emirates.

   d. Abu Dhabi is the capital and principal city of the United Arab Emirates.

6. Which of the following sentences is most conventional in spelling, punctuation, and mechanics?

   a. She has already read your letter and says your suggestion is alright with her.

   b. She has already read your letter and says your suggestion is all right with her.

   c. She has all ready read your letter and says your suggestion is alright with her.

   d. She has all ready read your letter and says your suggestion is all right with her.

7. Which of the following sentences is most conventional in spelling, punctuation, and mechanics?

   a. I'm sure you've perceived the new title occuring after my name.

b. I'm sure you've perceived the new title occurring after my name.

c. I'm sure you've percieved the new title occuring after my name.

d. I'm sure you've percieved the new title occurring after my name.

8. Which of the following sentences is most conventional in spelling, punctuation, and mechanics?

   a. In retracing his path, the courier was worryed that he might have omitted something.

   b. In retracing his path, the courier was worried that he might have omitted something.

   c. In retraceing his path, the courier was worryed that he might have omited something.

   d. In retraceing his path, the courier was worried that he might have omited something.

9. Which of the following sentences is most conventional in spelling, punctuation, and mechanics?

   a. The flag is red, green, white, and black.

   b. The flag is red, green, white and black.

   c. Both *a* and *b* are conventional.

   d. Neither *a* nor *b* is conventional.

10. Which of the following sentences is most conventional in spelling, punctuation, and mechanics?

    a. Did she complete the form marked "Secret"?

    b. Did she complete the form marked "Secret?"

    c. "Where do we go from here?" he asked.

    d. Both *a* and *c* are correct.

MANAGE YOUR WRITING *TODAY*

On the very next writing job you have to do, begin with some writing management: Remind yourself that you're a writer, that writing can be managed, and that it's largely a matter of managing time. Set up blocks of time for planning, drafting, and revising—with more time allocated for planning and revising than for drafting.

- Then call in your Internal Editor to make the best possible "assignment" for this writing task. Begin by spending five minutes "finding the 'we.'" Take another five minutes to ask yourself, "What is the smallest community to which my audience and I both belong?" and "How are my audience and I alike and different in the four PACK dimensions: personality, attitude, circumstances, and knowledge?" Spend another five minutes to "make holes, not drills" by defining the purpose of the piece of writing. Take another five minutes or so to "get your stuff together," to gather information for the piece of writing. Then end the planning stage with five minutes of "getting your ducks in a row," organizing your information to best achieve your purpose for your reader(s).

- Now "do it wrong the first time." Bring in your Internal Writer to draft your document with as little interference as possible from your Internal Editor.

- Then take a break—for as long as you can, but for at least five minutes. Use this time to gain some objectivity about your draft and to "change hats" from your Internal Writer's rumpled fedora to your Internal Editor's eyeshade.

- When you return from the break, try to trick yourself into thinking that someone else wrote the draft, and look at it as if you're seeing it for the first time. Then revise your document using all the tools you already have in your toolbox, as well as the tools you've learned so far in this course. Finish the revision stage by "finishing" the document, putting a professional surface on it with correct spelling, punctuation, and other mechanics.

When you've done that, take a few minutes to evaluate how the process worked for you. Evaluate especially whether "finishing the job" resulted in a more effective piece of writing at the end.

12

MANAGE YOUR WRITING
EVALUATE YOUR WRITING PROCESS

GOOD MANAGERS KNOW the importance of evaluating their work. As a manager of your own writing, you need to end each writing "hour" (as shown in Figure 12-1) with two or three minutes of evaluation—not of the written *product* (your Internal Editor has been doing that throughout the "revise" stage), but of your writing *process*. Which stages of the process needed more time than you gave them? Which stages needed less?

Like the hands on a clock, the writing process doesn't stop with each cycle. It's a continuous process. The evaluation you do at the end of one writing job can help you be a better manager at the beginning of the next.

I'm certainly not saying that your writing can become as mechanized as the writing of the executive at Ace Conveyor Company in Figure 12-2. But I am saying that in the past 36 hours you have learned a process that can let you manage, and streamline, your writing process in the way that engineers learn to streamline any other production process.

And through this recurring process, evaluated at the end of each cycle, you'll continue to grow as a writer for the rest of your life. You'll have learned to *manage your writing*.

MANAGE YOUR WRITING *TODAY*

On the very next writing job you have to do, begin with some writing management: Remind yourself that you're a writer, that writing can be managed, and that it's

FIGURE 12-1   Manage your writing.

FIGURE 12-2   Ace Conveyor Co.

largely a matter of managing time. Set up blocks of time for planning, drafting, and revising—with more time allocated for planning and revising than for drafting.

- Then call in your Internal Editor to make the best possible "assignment" for this writing task. Begin by spending five minutes "finding the 'we.'" Take another five minutes to ask yourself, "What is the smallest community to which my audience and I both belong?" and "How are my audience and I alike and different in the four PACK dimensions: personality, attitude, circumstances, and knowledge?" Spend another five minutes to "make holes, not drills" by defining the purpose of the piece of writing. Take another five minutes or so to "get your stuff together," to gather information for the piece of writing. Then end the planning stage with five minutes of "getting your ducks in a row," organizing your information to best achieve your purpose for your reader(s).
- Now "do it wrong the first time." Bring in your Internal Writer to draft your document with as little interference as possible from your Internal Editor.
- Then take a break—for as long as you can, but for at least five minutes. Use this time to gain some objectivity about your draft and to "change hats" from your Internal Writer's rumpled fedora to your Internal Editor's eyeshade.
- When you return from the break, try to trick yourself into thinking that someone else wrote the draft, and look at it as if you're seeing it for the first time. Then revise your document using all the tools you already have in your toolbox, as well as the tools you've learned so far in this book. Finish the revision stage by "finishing" the document, putting a professional surface on it with correct spelling, punctuation, and other mechanics.

When you've done that, take a few minutes to evaluate how the process worked for you. Did you take enough time at each stage? Too much time? Finally, evaluate whether managing your writing process resulted in a more effective piece of writing at the end.

MANAGE YOUR ONLINE WRITING

I N THE EARLY 1980s, when word processing software began to appear, Stewart Brand, father of the *Whole Earth Catalog*, called word processing the "technology I've been waiting half a lifetime for." Well, one short wait for that writer was one long wait for humankind. In the last 20 years, we have begun to use the most important new writing tool since the stylus—in fact, the only significantly new writing technology in 8,000 years—the computer.

Computer—what an ugly word, and what a misnomer. Von Neumann, back in the 1940s, had a better idea: He called the thing an "all-purpose machine." And the French, as usual, have a good word for it: *ordinateur*— the machine that orders, that organizes, that arranges. But *computer*? The word reduces one of humanity's most far-reaching inventions to a merely mathematical device.

Now don't get me wrong. I'm appropriately grateful to the mathematicians, engineers, and computer scientists who have worked to give us this tool. But they have done more than many of them know. The lasting value of their creation lies not in helping humanity to *compute* but in helping humanity to *write*.

THE WRITING MACHINE

Humanity has been writing, archeologists tell us, since about 6000 B.C. As mentioned briefly in the introduction, the first writers discovered that written language has several advantages over spoken language:

- It can be absorbed more quickly.
- It can be scanned with the eyes.
- It can be consulted later.
- It can be passed with confidence from messenger to messenger.

All these advantages are results of writing's relative *permanence*. But the very permanence that gives writing these advantages traditionally has made the process of creating it very difficult.

- First, the very physical act of representing an idea by a permanent squiggle—on stone, papyrus, slate, or paper—is so hard that few of us get really good at it. (Thank goodness you're not trying to read this book in my handwriting.) As a textbook once proclaimed in its title, writing is an unnatural act.
- And second, once we've made such a permanent squiggle, we're loath to change it.

As a result, most of us traditionally have worked very hard to get all those squiggles right the first time so that we don't have to do them again. As Figure I-1 illustrated, we agonize our way down the page, considering carefully each squiggle before we write it—planning, drafting, and editing all at once. And when the draft is finished, *we're* finished: The permanence of the squiggles traditionally has made us reluctant to look at them again (the literal meaning of *revise*) with an eye toward improvement.

The computer changes all this. It still gives us a permanent written product—on paper or disk—with all the advantages that permanence has had for 8,000 years. But—and this is important—it allows us to postpone the permanence until we want it, at the very end of the writing process. Until then, we can write on the most impermanent of media: a video screen.

The implications of this fact are profound at each stage of the writing process. At what this book is calling the "planning stage," we can begin by jotting down fragmentary ideas, copying notes from other sources, and roughing out possible organizational patterns. But with the computer, we can manipulate these jottings much more freely, arranging and combining them in new ways. And even more wonderfully, once we key in a word or phrase, we need never do so again, unless we wish to. Our preliminary jottings can become an actual part of our final document, in a way they never could when we composed on paper.

As we move into the "drafting phase" of the process, we can, if we wish, open our planning work in one window as we draft in another. When it's more efficient to move a phrase from one window to another than it is to rekey it, we can do that. And the anticipated ease of revision lets us draft much more freely and spontaneously than before, with much less constraint from what Chapter 6 calls our "Internal Editor."

It's at the revising stage that the computer really proves its worth as a writing machine. It allows us to do all the kinds of revising we could do on paper—deleting, inserting, and changing—but after each of these operations, we immediately have a "clean" copy of the document, not the very "dirty," marked-up copies we used to have. We can see exactly what we've done, instead of having to imagine it, so that we can make wiser editorial decisions.

The computer also permits other kinds of revision that were simply not possible on paper. A single command takes us to any given word. Another swaps any word or phrase for any other, either at all places it occurs or at those we select. And so on. When we're finally satisfied—or out of time—we can run spell-check. (And I'll beg you here to turn off the feature in your word processor that checks spelling as you type. Save spell-check for step 11.)

For all these reasons, the writing machine (call it a computer if you insist) directly supports and encourages the five-stage writing process that will make us more effective and efficient writers. With it, we have no excuse to remain sentence-by-sentence, "one stage" writers.

FOUR CHALLENGES

This book's introduction pointed out what you surely already knew: not only is most writing being done on computer, but more and more writing also is being read on computer screens—in the form of e-mail and Web pages. All the tools you've learned so far in this book certainly apply to online writing as much as they do to writing that's read on paper. But online writing brings its own special challenges. This appendix will look at four of those challenges and the ways that we writers must respond to them.

As also mentioned in the introduction, a study conducted by the Poynter Institute and Stanford University found that most readers of online news sites go first to the text; only 22 percent of readers look first at graphics. This is the reverse of how printed pages are read. So when we write for online readers, we need to make our text even more effective than when we write on paper.

The four challenges of online writing are shown in the left column of Figure A-1. They remind us that online writing is—or should be—screen-based, interactive, global, and immediate. Each of these challenges has implications:

- Implications for the "texture" of writing (its words, sentences, and paragraphs—the things we've learned to pay special attention to throughout the revising stage)
- Implications for the structure of writing (its overall organization—which we learned to pay special attention to at the end of the planning stage)

Online writing should be ▼	in texture	in structure
screen-based	• concise • highlighted	• visibly structured • "fronted"
interactive	• informatively linked	• "chunked" (but not linearly)
global	• multilingual, if possible • in "world English"	• multistructured, if possible (deductive and inductive)
immediate	• personal • objective, not "rhetorical"	• conversational • narrative
Manage Your Online Writing		

FIGURE A-1   Manage your online writing.

The first challenge of online writing is that it appears on screen. And according to Web usability expert Jakob Nielsen, screen-based reading (for now, at least) is 25 percent slower than paper-based reading. So as Figure A-1 points out, online writing should be especially concise. To use the language of Chapter 9, it should be especially economical because you're paying a lot for each word. Nielsen also has found that 79 percent of online readers scan rather than truly read. So online writing should be highlighted, with key words, sentences, or ideas accentuated by appearing in italic or boldface, for example.

Just as the texture of online writing has to meet the challenge of screen-based reading, so does its structure. Because online readers tend to scan, a Web page or an e-mail message should be visibly structured; it should have what Nielsen calls a "scannable layout." He found that the frequent use of headings and bullets can increase readability by 47 percent. And since only about 10 percent of online readers, in Nielsen's research, scroll below the text initially visible on the screen, online writing should be "fronted," with the most important information at the beginning. Unless you have a good reason otherwise—as in a "bad news" message, for example—structure your Web pages and e-mail messages like newspaper articles, with the most important information in the headline (or subject line) and the first paragraph.

The second challenge of online writing is that it should be interactive. Words on paper can't appear or disappear immediately at the reader's command, but words on a computer screen can. So readers of online text increasingly expect it to be interactive. So in its texture, online writing should be informatively linked, giving its readers clear choices to make about where to go next. As Nielsen says, "The departure page must include sufficient information to enable users to decide what link to follow next." He adds that link titles should include "details about the kind of information to be found on the destination page, as well as how it relates to the anchor text and to the context of the current page."

Making online text interactive requires "chunking" it, that is, splitting it into shorter passages. These chunks, however, should not be merely linear, turning the computer into nothing more than an expensive page-turning machine. Readers expect that online writing, especially Web-based writing, will give them true choices.

The third challenge of online writing is that it should be global. The universality of the Web means that readers can represent dozens or hundreds of cultures. And even an e-mail message to one person can be easily forwarded to many more around the world. So if you want or expect a global readership for your writing, especially on Web pages, consider making it multilingual. If you can't get it translated into multiple languages, at least translate it yourself into "world" English—English that relies on relatively simple words and sentences and that avoids analogies specific to one culture, such as the doughnuts and muffins of Chapter 1. Naturally, by translating your draft into "world" English, you'll almost always be making it more effective for native English speakers within your own culture as well.

Besides requiring simpler words and sentences, global readers also come to your writing with different structural preferences and expectations. Ronald Scollon and Suzanne Wong Scollon, in their book, *Intercultural Communication*, remind us that some readers prefer deductive organization, with the topic "introduced at the beginning so that it will be clear what the relevance of the supporting arguments is." Other readers prefer inductive organization, with the supporting arguments first, building up to a conclusion. Although both patterns are used in all societies, some societies may have a general preference for one or the other. Although I know of no examples yet, the interactive nature of the Web gives us the opportunity to create multi-structured text, with both deductive and inductive options for our readers.

The fourth challenge of online writing is that readers expect it to be immediate—without "mediation." As the writers of *The Cluetrain Manifesto* say, "The Internet became a place where people could talk to other people without constraint. Without filters or censorship or official sanction." So the texture of online writing should be personal, not bureaucratic. Nielsen's research found that on Web pages, "what's respected is the presence of a clear voice." *The Cluetrain Manifesto*, again, talks about voices, comparing the business voice, "virtually the same as everyone else's," with the personal voice, the "strongest, most direct expression of who we are."

Similarly, online writing generally should be objective, not "rhetorical" or hyped. As Nielsen says, "The Web is a rather 'cool' medium that encourages the use of facts with links to back-up datasheets and detailed numbers. You cannot get away with the superficial hyperbole that may work in television commercials or magazine advertising."

In its structure, online writing should meet the challenge of immediacy by being conversational, by respecting the reader's time by being relevant, by providing as much information as the reader needs but no more, and by telling the truth.

Online writing also should make extensive use of narratives—of stories. Stories have always been important in forming communities and organizations. As *The Cluetrain Manifesto* reminds us, "Stories play a large part in the success of organizations. With stories, we teach, pass along knowledge of our craft to colleagues, and create a sense of shared mission." Bran Ferren, an executive vice president of Walt Disney Imagineering, told a writer for *CIO Web Business Magazine*, "The Web is a storytelling medium. Most people function in a storytelling mode. It's the way we communicate ideas, richly." He continued, "The deeper memory of an organization has to do with the sense of community, colleagues functioning together, history, accomplishments and so forth. All of that ultimately makes up the culture of a corporation. Part of the issue is how to convey that to the outside world. Information technology is now being used to do that in the Web pages that many companies are now using, and they're doing it incredibly badly because they're not taking it seriously as a storytelling problem."

MANAGE YOUR GLOBAL WRITING

THE CASE OF THE BELGIAN FRENCH FRIES*

Y OU'RE A U.S. BUSINESSPERSON who's just begun negotiations in Antwerp. Your Belgian counterparts have taken you to lunch at an outdoor café. When the food comes, one of them turns to you and says, "Have some of these french fries; they're so much better than the terrible fries you have in America!" How do you respond?

As business becomes more global, more and more business people find themselves communicating internationally. This communication is taking place at all levels of organizations. For example, at one of our client companies, a U.S. insurance firm owned by a five-nation European alliance, nearly 20 percent of all employees reported communicating outside their continent more than once a month, mostly in writing.

When businesspeople communicate internationally, they bring to that communication their own communication styles. We suggest that four such styles are prevalent in international business communication. By understanding

*This article, by Kenneth W. Davis, Teun De Rycker, and J. Piet Verckens, appeared, in a revised form, in the October 1997 issue of *Global Workforce* magazine.

these four styles, and by recognizing them in ourselves and others, we can all become more effective global communicators, in speech and in writing—and help ourselves and our organizations survive and thrive in the growing world market.

A COMMUNICATION GRID

In his book, *The Seven Habits of Highly Effective People,* Stephen R. Covey argues that all our interactions are colored by the amount of consideration we have for the feelings and convictions of others and by the amount of "courage" we have in embodying our own feelings and convictions. He graphs these two variables against each other in a grid that defines four styles—or "paradigms"—of human interaction.

Covey suggests that in low-consideration, low-courage transactions, both parties lose. By not having the courage of our own feelings and convictions, we don't get what we want, and by not considering the feelings and convictions of others, we are not able to give them what they want.

Similarly, low-consideration, high-courage transactions are attempts at "win-lose" bargaining, and high-consideration, low-courage transactions are attempts at the reverse. We say "attempts" because, as Covey argues, one party in an interaction cannot truly win unless the other party wins as well. Covey's grid shows that "win-win" transactions take place only when we bring a paradigm of both high consideration and high courage.

We have found that these same four styles dominate international business communication. That is, the same grid can be used to define the four main kinds of international business communicators: "isolationist," "ugly tourist," "gone native," and "global communicator"—as shown in Figure B-1.

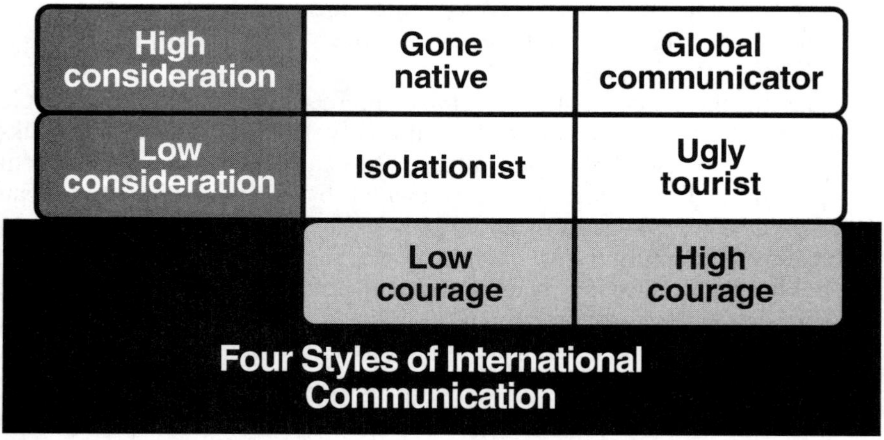

High consideration	Gone native	Global communicator
Low consideration	Isolationist	Ugly tourist
	Low courage	High courage

Four Styles of International Communication

FIGURE B-1 Four styles of international communication.

In the lower-left cell of the grid is the "isolationist." Isolationist communicators bring a low embodiment of their own cultural identity, their own feelings and convictions, and they bring a low consideration for the cultural identities of others. As a result, real communication never takes place.

In the lower-right cell is the "ugly tourist." The phrase is adapted from the title of William J. Lederer's novel *The Ugly American*. The book's title has become a common phrase for a certain kind of American when traveling overseas, one with a high assertion of his own culture but with a low consideration for the host culture—complaining loudly, for example, that "you can't get a good hamburger in Tokyo." However, our phrase *ugly tourist* reflects the fact that such behavior is not restricted to Americans.

Far too many businesspeople fall into this category, asserting strongly their own culture, their own business agenda, but not recognizing the culture or agenda of others. They work hard for a "win," but by not allowing their international partners to win as well, they lose in the long run. They tend to see the world through their own cultural filters without being aware of those filters.

For example, we talked with a Canadian businesswoman who complained that the Dutch with whom she deals answer her questions with too much information. "When I ask what was the 1994 price, I expect to get the 1994 price, no more," she said. However, in the same interview, she called the European belief that North Americans are too literal "not a fair characterization."

In the upper-left cell is the paradigm we call "gone native." The phrase probably originated in the days of the British Empire to describe a foreign service officer who became so immersed in the local culture that he stopped being of service to the Crown.

The temptation to "go native" always exists for the modern international businessperson as well. In any company, people with international interests tend to be attracted to international positions. Such positions, in any country's corporations, are occupied by more than their share of Anglophiles, Francophiles, "Japanophiles," or "Americophiles." And we've all heard the advice, "When in Rome, do as the Romans do."

This kind of high consideration for others' cultures is desirable in international businesspeople. But when it is coupled, as in this cell of the grid, with low embodiment of one's own culture and one's own interests, the result is a "lose-win" bargain, ultimately no bargain at all

THE GLOBAL COMMUNICATOR

We suggest, of course, that the most effective paradigm lies in the upper-right cell of the grid. We call this paradigm the "global communicator," the businessperson who brings high consideration for others' culture but also the high courage of accepting her own culture.

We interviewed such a global communicator, a Portuguese business-man working in Amsterdam on the creation of structures for sharing knowl-edge across a multinational company. This manager clearly asserted his own culture; he seemed proud of being Portuguese as he spoke of his culture's distinctive characteristics. But he also spoke admiringly of the strengths of the other cultures represented in the company.

His high-consideration, high-courage paradigm emerged for us most clearly when we asked if he liked being greeted in Portuguese before switching to English, the working language of his company. "Yes," he said, "it's a nice token gesture. But attitude is more important—to be a joyful per-son, to be open-minded. And there are other ways to convey that attitude."

USING THE GRID

So back to that Antwerp café and to the challenge: "Have some of these french fries; they're so much better than the terrible fries you have in America!" How do you respond? The grid suggests four possible ways.

If you're an isolationist, you ignore the challenge and say nothing. Perhaps you change the subject. Conflict is avoided, but communication doesn't happen. The result is lose-lose.

If you're an ugly tourist, you rise to the bait. "Are you kidding? You call these french fries? In America we wouldn't feed these to a pig." In the right relationship, built over time, a good laugh may follow. But in most cases, the result will be win-lose. You've satisfied your offended honor but lost a chance to build a relationship.

If you've gone native, you roll over and play dead. "You're absolutely right," you say. "These are much better than we have in the States." You may have ingratiated yourself with your hosts, but you've probably diminished yourself in their eyes. The lose-win result has no long-term payoff.

But if you're a global communicator, you say something like, "Ah, I'm sorry that you haven't found good french fries in the United States. Next time you're there, I hope you'll let me take you where you can get some very good ones. Or better yet, I hope you'll let me treat you to some more typically American food. But meanwhile, I certainly enjoy these fries; they're very good indeed!"

The result is win-win. You've shown the courage of your own convic-tions and a consideration for your hosts' culture. Even more important, you've opened a door to furthering your relationship.

So give the grid a try. Use it to examine your international commu-nication, both spoken and written. With practice, you'll become a global communicator.

MANAGE YOUR SPEAKING

O F ALL THE WAYS to communicate, speaking seems the most feared by the most people. In a survey I conducted of more than a hundred business leaders, they named "speaking to a group" as their biggest communication problem. In fact, speaking received more than twice as many first-place votes as the runner-up problem.

Not all fear is bad, of course. Controlled nervousness, even fear, can give a vital energy, an edge, to a presentation. No speech is worse than that of the speaker who has absolutely no fear, who too obviously regards the presentation as a routine chore to get through. This may well be the cause of the response faced by Manager Fred Barnwall in Figure C-1.

But there's no reason to let speaking remain a number-one communication problem for you. You can learn to manage your speaking like you manage your writing—or any other business process. Whether you're giving a formal speech to hundreds of listeners or an informal briefing to two or three, you can become less afraid and more effective by taking charge of your preparation process.

To do so, use the same tools—with slightly different emphasis—that you're learning to use in this course to become a five-stage writer, as shown in Figure C-2.

Start by managing, by allocating available time. Then begin a planning stage by "finding the 'we,'" the community to which you and your audience both belong. "PACK" for the journey by asking yourself what personality traits, attitudes, circumstances, and knowledge you and your audience share. Then ask yourself what special personality traits, attitudes, circumstances, and knowledge you have that bring you before this audience. Your answers

FIGURE C-1   Manager Fred Barnwall senses a mood shift among his salespeople.

FIGURE C-2   Five-stage writing.

to these questions will help you feel "at home" with your listeners but also qualified to stand before them.

Then "make holes, not drills." Look beyond the speech to the purpose you want it to achieve. Will your presentation function as conversation, correspondence, covenant, or conception for your audience? Start visualizing not the presentation itself but what will happen after it's over. Picture your audience leaving the room filled with new knowledge and new attitudes. Picture them putting your ideas to work in their jobs.

Now start "getting your stuff together," gathering the content of your presentation. Ask the "who," "what," "where," "when," "why," and "how" questions that will lead you to the information you need. Try mind-mapping your content. Remember, however, that a reasonably timed oral presentation has room for far less information than a written one. So, for example, instead of the three examples you might use in a report, choose the one best example for your speech.

Then "get your ducks in a row," organizing your material into the best order to achieve your purpose. This step is even more important for speaking than for writing: readers of a badly organized memo or letter can at least skip around to reorganize it in their minds, but listeners to a badly organized speech are stuck with what they're getting. So decide carefully what you want to say first, second, third, and so on.

Now that you've planned your presentation, you're at the main decision point. Will you actually write your speech, or will you speak from notes or an outline? Choose wisely based on your purpose and on the circumstances of the presentation. A written speech is generally for more formal occasions, of course—but not always. Even if the occasion is relatively informal, written remarks can have great impact, showing you as competent and committed to what you're saying. And a written script, even if you never actually read from it, can help to reduce stage fright by providing "insurance."

If you speak from notes or an outline, tailor them to your needs. Include key words and reminders of key anecdotes or examples. In particular, include reminders of the organization of your presentation so that there's no chance of your getting lost. If you've mind-mapped your speech, consider using your mind map itself as an outline at the podium.

If you go ahead and write your speech, consider putting individual sentences on separate cards—or separated by white space on sheets of paper. As James C. Humes points out in his book, *The Sir Winston Method*, Winston Churchill perfected the method of reading each sentence to himself silently and then making eye contact with his audience and repeating that sentence aloud. The pauses, far from becoming distracting, can add drama to a more formal speech and make you seem thoughtful and deliberate.

Whether you write your presentation or give it from notes, be sure to emphasize the "turn signals" that let your listeners know where you're going next. Transition words and phrases like *therefore, however,* and *next* are even more important in speaking than in writing; your listeners can't look ahead, after all. Also more important in speaking than in writing are "saying what you mean," "paying by the word," and "translating into English." Again, listeners, unlike readers, can't stop to figure out what you mean.

As the introduction said, information technologies are bringing new importance to the written word. But writing will never completely replace speaking in business or anywhere else. So learn to manage your speaking process. You can become an effective—and almost fearless—speaker.

A P P E N D I X

RESOURCES FOR MANAGING YOUR WRITING

BOOKS ON COMMUNICATION IN BUSINESS

Several recent popular books stress the growing importance of communication in business. Among the best are

- *The Brand You 50,* by Tom Peters. This small book, one of a trilogy called *Reinventing Work*, offers 50 tools for becoming a "brand," whether as an entrepreneur or as an employee.
- *The Cluetrain Manifesto: The End of Business as Usual,* by Rick Levine, Christopher Locke, Doc Searls, and David Weinberger. Born on a Web site, this book signals what I predict will eventually be seen as the biggest change in the history of business communication—the change discussed, in connection with this book, in Appendix A.
- *Good Business: Leadership, Flow, and the Making of Meaning,* by Mihaly Csikszentmihalyi. The psychologist who gave us the "flow" model discussed in Chapter 5 applies that model broadly to the leadership of organizations.
- *Information Anxiety 2*, by Richard Saul Wurman. The father of "information architecture" beautifully displays specific strategies for fighting the war against "infoglut."

- *Leading Out Loud: Inspiring Change through Authentic Communication,* by Terry Pearce. A leading executive coach presents a remarkably deep and broad discussion of leading through communicating with integrity.
- *On Communicating,* by Mark H. McCormack. The famed sports marketer shares his street smarts on effective business communication.
- *What to Say to Get What You Want,* by Sam Deep and Lyle Sussman. Almost all business communication guides give us the "how" of speaking and writing. This book gives us the "what" by portraying 44 types of bosses, employees, coworkers, and customers and advising us on what to say to each.

DICTIONARIES

Be careful when you choose a dictionary: small paperbacks generally aren't complete enough for business writers, and many hardback dictionaries are out of date or badly edited—even many that carry the name *Webster's*, which isn't a trademark. Fortunately, several reliable hardback "desk" dictionaries are available. I recommend

- *The American Heritage Dictionary of the English Language.* The most attractive and readable of the major dictionaries, with particular strengths in word histories and usage.
- *Merriam-Webster's Collegiate Dictionary.* The most widely used desk dictionary.

THESAURUSES

Using a thesaurus is risky. It can help you find a word you know but have forgotten. However, it can hurt you by suggesting a word that isn't appropriate or effective for your specific need. My favorites are

- *The American Heritage College Thesaurus*
- *Bartlett's Roget's Thesaurus*

USAGE GUIDES

Usage guides cover the etiquette of language from when you can split infinitives to whether you can say *prioritize.* Of the many usage guides available, I recommend

- *Merriam-Webster's Dictionary of English Usage*

WRITING GUIDES

Surely no book on writing has been more recommended than "Strunk and White." Some of its reputation is undeserved: *The Elements of Style* too often leans toward academic stuffiness and away from practicality. For example, a William Faulkner sentence containing the words *gutful, mendicant,* and *thrall* is described as using "ordinary" words. The book is saved, however, by its solid advice and engaging style. It makes for enjoyable reading, with some learning in the process. But several more useful options are available, especially as supplements to this *36-Hour Course*:

- *The Business Writer's Handbook,* by Gerald J. Alred, Charles T. Brusaw, and Walter E. Oliu. This A–Z reference book can answer lots of specific questions at each step in the writing process.
- *The Elements of Business Writing: A Guide to Writing Clear, Concise Letters, Memos, Reports, Proposals, and Other Business Documents,* by Gary Blake and Robert W. Bly. This book, with an obvious nod to Strunk and White, lists 67 principles of good writing, with about two pages each of details and examples.
- *Revising Business Prose,* by Richard Lanham. Taking the same basic approach to revision as I do, this book has gained wide recognition for its "paramedic method" of revising.
- *Style: Ten Lessons in Clarity and Grace,* by Joseph M. Williams. Although it doesn't focus on business writing, Williams's book is another excellent resource for revision.
- *The Writing Coach,* by Lee Clark Johns. This large-format book, by a leading writing consultant, is dedicated "to everyone who 'writes for a living'—which means almost all working adults."

OTHER BOOKS

Two other books, though not directly focused on writing, present two of the most useful sets of tools I use as a business writer:

- *Getting Things Done: The Art of Stress-Free Productivity*, by David Allen. Allen's book, the source for the "law of the next action" in my book's introduction, has been invaluable in helping me to learn to manage my writing—and much of the rest of my life.
- *The Mind Map Book,* by Tony Buzan with Barry Buzan. Written by the great popularizer of mind-mapping, this beautifully illustrated book is still the best introduction to the subject.

WEB RESOURCES

Because Web pages come and go often, this book doesn't list any. However, you can find an up-to-date page of recommended links at http://www.ManageYourWriting.com.

ANSWER KEY TO EXERCISES

CHAPTER 1

1. *c.* All other decisions at the planning stage depend on your sense of community with your reader(s) and your sense of the ways in which you and your reader(s) are alike and different.

2. *c.* Communication requires community, and community requires communication.

3. *b.* Consider the smallest possible community to which you and your audience both belong. The smaller your shared community, the more information you'll have about similarities and differences with your audience.

4. *c.* Both similarities and differences should be considered.

5. *b.* Considering both your own personality and that of your reader(s) will allow you to make an effective adjustment for the needs of your reader(s).

6. *d.* Avoiding sentimentally, supporting your opinions logically, and making your thinking process clear are all important when communicating with a "thinker."

7. *a.* Similarities and differences between your attitudes and those of your audience definitely should be considered at the planning stage.

8. *b.* Maslow's hierarchy can help you to assess how your writing can fill a need for your reader(s).

9. *c.* It is most helpful to visualize your reader(s) reading and reacting to your message.

10. *a.* COIK material ("Clear Only If Known") will be understandable by the reader(s) only if the reader(s) already knows it.

CHAPTER 2

1. *c.* Defining purpose should be done after defining writer and reader(s) but before collecting and organizing information for your message.
2. *c.* Subject lines were invented for filing purposes, and they invite generality and vagueness.
3. *c.* "Purpose"-defining subject lines are helpful to both the writer and the reader.
4. *b.* Readers always want to know "What's in it for me?"
5. *d.* *Ko* and *mei,* the roots for communication and community, mean "together" and "change."
6. *c.* Most pieces of communication have both *ko* (community-building) and *mei* (change-producing) functions.
7. *c.* A mission statement has a longer-term "covenant" purpose.
8. *a.* A birthday card has a *ko,* "conversation" purpose.
9. *d.* A monthly profit-and-loss statement has a shorter-term purpose.
10. *c.* A corporate history, in its focus on the past, has a *ko,* "covenant" purpose.

CHAPTER 3

1. *c.* Gathering information should be done after defining audience and purpose but before organizing the information.
2. *d.* Information gathering should be done before drafting to reduce interruptions during drafting, to reduce the possibility of leaving out important information, and to give you the confidence to draft more easily—as well as to focus carefully on your information.
3. *c.* *Who, what, where, when, why,* and *how* questions are usually most effective.
4. *c.* The reporter's checklist can be valuable at both the planning and revising stages.
5. *b.* The four pairs of questions are based on the words *same/different, whole/parts, time/space,* and *cause/effect.*
6. *b.* During an interview, you should listen to the responses you get and ask follow-up questions.
7. *c.* Web-based information can be accurate or inaccurate, so it should be read and used critically.
8. *c.* While brainstorming, don't be concerned about whether or not you'll eventually be able to use a particular idea in the piece of writing.
9. *d.* None of the statements about mind-mapping is true.

10. *b.* The writing you do at the information-gathering stage should be based on the definitions of audience and purpose you've made in steps 1 and 2, but it need not be spelled and punctuated correctly, nor carefully organized, at this point.

CHAPTER 4

Exercise A

1. *c.* Organizing information should be done after defining audience and purpose and after gathering information but before drafting.

2. *d.* Organizing information should be done before drafting in order to allow you to focus on the best order for the reader, to reduce interruptions during drafting, and to turn the drafting job into a series of smaller jobs.

3. *b.* Writing is difficult in part because it requires converting nonlinear thinking into linear words, sentences, and paragraphs.

4. *a.* One-stage writers tend to write things down in the order in which they think of them.

5. *c.* Formal outlines should be used at the planning stage only if they are useful to the writer.

6. *b.* Routine requests for information generally should begin with the request itself, phrased as a question if possible.

7. *d.* Claims generally should begin with a statement of the problem.

8. *b.* Good-news responses generally should begin with the good news.

9. *c.* Bad-news responses generally should begin with a neutral acknowledgment.

10. *a.* Indirect persuasion usually does not begin with a statement of the writer's position.

Exercise B

This letter has no single best organizational pattern. The following is how I probably would organize it. Compare your answers with mine, and if we disagree, see how you would defend your plan. Taking the time, at the planning stage, to think about organization is more important than coming up with a particular "correct" plan.

1. *b*
2. *h* (or *a*)
3. *a* (or *h*)
4–7. *c, f, i,* and *e* (or *i, e, c,* and *f* or some other combinations)
8. *d*
9. *g*

CHAPTER 6

1. *b.* Overall organization decisions should be made in step 4 in the planning stage.
2. *d.* Spell-checking should be done at the revising stage.
3. *d.* Decisions about words should be postponed until the revising stage.
4. *c.* You should devote the drafting stage to putting sentences down on paper or computer screen.
5. *b.* The purpose of your document should be determined in step 2 in the planning stage.
6. *a.* At the managing stage, you allocate time for the other stages.
7. *b.* Decisions about starting and ending the document should be made in step 4 in the planning stage.
8. *d.* Reviewing paragraphs for transitions should be done at the revising stage.
9. *b.* You should get an initial sense of your audience in step 1 in the planning stage.
10. *b.* Information collecting should be done in step 3 in the planning stage.

CHAPTER 7

Exercise A

1. *b.* The two sentences have a *but* relationship, with the second qualifying the first.
2. *c.* The two sentences have an *and* relationship and can be combined effectively.
3. *d.* The first sentence has a *colon* relationship with the second and third, which have an *and* relationship with each other. All three can be combined effectively.
4. *a.* The two sentences have a *but* relationship, with the second qualifying the first.
5. *c.* The first sentence is the result of the second, so they can be combined with the word *because*.
6. *d.* The two sentences have a *so* relationship, with the first stating the cause of the second.
7. *b.* The two sentences have an *and* relationship and can be combined effectively. Answers *c* and *d* would work well if the word *also* were added.
8. *d.* Answers *c* and *d* both express the correct *and* relationship, but answer *d* does so more economically.
9. *d.* The two sentences have a *because* relationship, with the first sentence expressing the result of the second.

10. *b.* The two sentences have a *colon* relationship. The first sentence makes a general statement, and the second provides specifics.

Exercise B

Answers will vary, but here's one possible revision:

> In the past, procedures for repair and calibration of test equipment have been unsatisfactory. Too much time has been spent taking instruments to and from Instrument Services, and some equipment has been misplaced.
>
> Beginning November 10, "drop zones" will be used for the pickup of test equipment. Instruments that need calibration or repair may be taken to the appropriate drop zone, as shown on the attached list. Instruments will be picked up Mondays and Thursdays.
>
> Managers or their representatives will be responsible for taking equipment to drop zones; Instrument Services personnel will return them. To ensure that instruments are returned to the correct manager, mark the correct department and building number on each instrument before taking it to the drop zone.
>
> To find out whether an instrument has been repaired or calibrated, or for more information on the drop zone system, call Instrument Services, not the drop zone coordinator.

CHAPTER 8

Exercise A

1. *b.* This sentence is active and has a real subject (*We*) and a real verb (*can't participate*) in the subject and verb positions.

2. *a.* This sentence has real verbs (*need* and *understand*) in both its clauses. The other three sentences hide these verbs.

3. *c.* This sentence focuses on the reader instead of the writer, and it has real verbs (*determine* and *benefit*) in both its clauses.

4. *c.* This sentence has a real subject (*expenses*), not an empty subject (*It* or *There*).

5. *d.* This sentence has real subjects (*I* and *issues*) in both its clauses.

6. *b.* This sentence has a real subject (*headquarters*) instead of an empty subject (*there*).

7. *b.* This sentence has a real subject (*I*) in its main clause and a real verb (*submit*) in its subordinate clause.

8. *a.* This sentence has both a real subject (*course*) and a real verb (*will examine*).

9. *d.* This sentence is active, with a real verb (*canceled*).

10. *a.* This sentence has a real subject (*process*).

Exercise B

Answers will vary, but here's one possible revision:

> In recent weeks several of you have made public statements about our company, statements that I believe are harmful to C&E's public image.
>
> I referred this matter to the Board of Directors, who discussed it at some length and decided that in the future, all public statements about our company must be cleared in advance by our office, on forms available.
>
> I appreciate your cooperation.

CHAPTER 9

Exercise A

1. *d*
2. *b*
3. *d*
4. *c*
5. *c*
6. *c*
7. *b*
8. *d*
9. *b*
10. *c*

Exercise B

Answers will vary, but here's one possible revision:

> The following changes have been made to our vacation policy:
>
> - April 1, our founder's birthday, will become a company holiday. We hope this extra holiday will increase morale.
> - We have arranged with a travel agency to provide reduced-price vacation opportunities. Their brochure, listing all tours, is available in the Personnel Office.
> - All managers must report employee vacation preferences quarterly.
>
> Thank you. Please call me if you have questions.

CHAPTER 10

Exercise A

1. *d*
2. *b*
3. *c*
4. *a*
5. *d*
6. *b*
7. *d*
8. *d*
9. *b*
10. *c*

Exercise B

Answers will vary, but here's one possible revision:

> As I've talked with many of you over the past several months, I've often heard you ask, "Are we trying to produce too many new products? Do we really need such a large line?"
>
> My first response is to stress the importance of changing our company's image. To get our market share, we must correct the faults of the past. We must be seen as a company willing to innovate.
>
> *[The last sentence probably should be eliminated. Consider the negative effect of simplifying it into something like "I'm sure that if you look into the matter, you will find that I am right."]*

CHAPTER 11

1. *a.* The possessive pronoun *its* (like the possessive pronouns *his, hers,* and *yours*) is spelled without an apostrophe. The word spelled *it's* is a contraction of *it is*.
2. *d.* The phrase *a lot* is spelled as two words. In the United States, periods and commas always go inside closing quotation marks.
3. *b.* *Stationery*, meaning "writing paper," is spelled with an *e*. Words ending in two consonants, such as *print*, don't double a consonant when adding a suffix.
4. *d.* *Effect*, as a noun, means "a result." *Affect*, as a noun, is a fairly uncommon psychological term. *Effect*, as a verb, means "to bring about," as in "The prisoner effected an escape." *Affect*, as a verb, means "to influence."

5. *d.* *Capital,* with an *a,* is a city; *capitol,* with an *o,* is a building. *Principle* is a "fundamental concept"; *principal,* as a noun or adjective, means "chief."

6. *b.* The phrase *all ready* means "everyone or everything ready." The word *already* means "by now." *Alright* is an unconventional spelling of the phrase *all right.*

7. *b.* *Perceived* is spelled with an *ei*; as the verse says, "*I* before *e* except after *c.*" (And remember, there are a few exceptions even to that.) Words such as *occur,* ending with one vowel followed by one consonant in an accented syllable, usually double that consonant before suffixes beginning with a vowel.

8. *b.* Words such as *retrace,* ending in a silent *e,* usually drop that *e* before a suffix beginning with a vowel. Words such as *worry,* ending in a consonant plus a *y,* usually change the *y* to *i* before a suffix. *Omit* follows the same rule as *occur* in answer 7.

9. *c.* Book publishers generally use a comma before the conjunction in a series. Newspaper publishers generally do not. Both are conventional in their own contexts. Just be consistent. (And if you really want me to give you an answer, well, okay, use the comma.)

10. *d.* Question marks (and exclamation points) go inside closing quotation marks if they are part of the quoted material. If, on the other hand, they give their meaning to the entire sentence outside the quotation marks, they go outside the closing quotation marks.

INDEX

Actions today
  break stage, 106–107
  draft stage, 92–93
  economical writing, 143
  finishing writing, 173
  information management, 64–65
  information structure, 82–83
  paragraph management, 121–122
  purpose management, 53
  reader relationship, 38–39
  sentence economy, 143
  structure management, 82–83
  subject and verb management, 133–134
  word choice management, 164–165
  writing management overview, 21
Active voice, 128–129
Asking questions, information management, 57–59
Attitude, reader relationship, 29–32, 189–190
Audience (*See* Reader relationship, planning stage)

Bad-news response, information structure, 76–77
Blogs, 8
Books, as resource, 193–194
Break, five-stage writing, 95–107
  actions today, 106–107
  exercise, 104–106
  to gain distance, 95–98
  internal writer vs. internal editor, 100–104

Break, five-stage writing (*Cont.*):
  overview, 19
  shift to reader-based writing, 98–99

Changing minds, 77–79
Circumstances in reader relationship, 32–35, 189–190
Claims, information structure, 75–76
Clear Only If Known (COIK), 36
COIK (Clear Only If Known), 36
Collecting data, 55–57, 60–61, 74–75
Common sense and economical writing, 137–139
Communication
  community created by, 25–27
  global grid, 186–187
  knowledge economy, 5
  Ko-mei grid, 48–51
  long-term and short-term, 47–51
  oral vs. written, 7–8
  third wave, 5–6
  writing management overview, 2–6
Community, reader relationship, 25–27
Competence in writing, 9–10
Complex language, word choice, 153–155, 159–161
Compliance factors, 79
Computers and writing, 179–181
Conception communication, 51
Confidence in writing performance, 10, 11

Consideration, global communication, 186–187,
    188
Context, reader relationship, 25–27
Conversation communication, 49, 51
Courage, global communication, 186–187, 188
Covenant communication, 50
Craft, writing as, 12–13
Culture and communication, 6, 26, 35–36,
    181–188
Customers, 25
    (*See also* Reader relationship, planning stage)

Data collection, 55–57, 60–61, 74–75
Debriefing, draft management, 88–89
Default value, 35
Dictionaries, as resource, 194
Discipline, 13
Distance, break stage, 95–98
Drafting, five-stage writing, 85–93
    actions today, 92–93
    computer writing, 180
    debriefing exercise, 88–89
    draft as prototype, 86–87, 96–97
    exercise, 88–92
    "flow," 90–92
    overview, 20
    "quick and dirty" draft, 19, 85–93
    speaking, 191
    writer's block, 89
    in writing process, 14, 15, 19

E-mail address of author, 12
Economical writing, revising stage, 135–143
    actions today, 143
    exercises, 140–143
    importance of, 135–137
    objectivity and common sense, 137–139
    overview, 19
    prepositions, 139–140
    revising for, 137–139
    simplicity is best, 152–156
    "which-hunt," 139
Economy, defined, 135–136
Editor, internal, 100–104
English, translate into (*See* Word choice
    management, revising stage)
English word origins, 149–153
Evaluation stage, 18, 20, 175–177
Exercises
    answers to, 197–204
    break stage, 104–106
    draft stage, 88–92

Exercises (*Cont.*):
    economical writing, 140–143
    finishing writing, 171–173
    information management, 63–64
    information structure, 80–82
    paragraph management, 118–121
    purpose management, 51–53
    reader relationship, 36–38
    sentence economy, 140–143
    subject and verb management, 131–133
    word choice management, 161–164

Finishing, revising stage, 167–173
    actions today, 173
    awareness and proofing, 167–170
    exercise, 171–173
    overview, 18, 20
    speaking, 192
First wave communication, 3, 7
Five-stage writing
    break stage, 95–107
    drafting stage, 85–93
    overview, 14–15, 17–20
    planning stage, 23–83
    revision stage, 109–173
    and speaking, 189–192
    summary, 19–20
"Flow" state, 90–92
Formulas, 73–77, 156–159
Four pairs questions, 58–59
French word origins, 152–153

Germanic word origins, 149–153
Global communication, 6, 26, 35–36, 181–188
Good-news response, information structure, 76
Grammar, revising stage, 167–173
Grids, communication, 48–51, 186–187

Hidden subjects and verbs, 124–128
Hierarchy of needs, Maslow's, 31–32
History of words, 149–153

Immediate, online writing as, 181–184
Information management, planning stage, 55–65
    actions today, 64–65
    asking questions, 57–59
    data collection, 55–57, 60–61, 74–75
    exercise, 63–64
    interviews, 60
    mind-mapping, 61–62
    planning stage overview, 19
Information society, 2–6

Information structure, planning stage, 67–83
  actions today, 82–83
  changing minds, 77–79
  data collection, 55–57, 60–61, 74–75
  example, 67–83, 69–71
  exercises, 80–82
  formulas, 73–77
  information to knowledge, 79–80
  organizing techniques, 72–73
  persuasion, 77–79
  planning stage overview, 19
  thought into linear writing, 67–69
Interactive, online writing as, 181–184
Internal customer, 25
Internal writer/editor, 100–104
International communication, 6, 26, 35–36,
  181–188
Internet
  online writing management, 8, 179–184
  web-based resources, 196
  web site of author, 11, 12, 196
Interviews, 60
IRS word choice example, 147–149

Knowledge
  information structure, 79–80
  process knowledge, 10, 11
  reader relationship, 35–36, 189–190
  writing in knowledge economy, 1, 3–4, 6–8
Ko and *mei* communication, 26, 46–47, 48–51

Latinate word origins, 150–154
Law of next action, 16–18
Linear writing structure, 67–69
Long-term communication, 47–51

Managing and evaluation stage, 18, 20, 175–177
Managing your writing (*See* Writing manage-
  ment overview; *specific topics*)
Maslow's hierarchy of needs, 31–32
MBTI (Myers-Briggs Type Indicator), 28–29
Mechanics, revising stage, 167–173
Mei and *ko* communication, 26, 46–47, 48–51
Memo redesign, 44–46
Mind-mapping, 61–62
Modifiers, subject and verb management,
  129–131
Myers-Briggs Type Indicator (MBTI), 28–29

Obfuscating language, word choice, 153–155,
  159–161
Objectivity, 95–98, 137–139, 184

Online (*See* Internet)
Oral communication, 7–8, 189–192
Order of presented information (*See* Information
  structure, planning stage)

PACK (personality, attitude, circumstances, and
  knowledge), 28–36, 189–190
Paragraph management, revising stage,
  109–122
  actions today, 121–122
  chunking, online, 183
  exercises, 118–121
  overview, 19
  revision importance, 109–110
  revision tools, 6, 110–112, 123–124
  sentence management for, 112–118, 191–192
  (*See also* Revising, five-stage writing)
Passive voice, 128–129
Performance of writing, 9–11
Permanence of writing, 7–8, 180
Personality of reader, 27–29, 189–190
Persuasion in writing structure, 77–79
Planning, five-stage writing, 23–83
  computer writing, 180
  information management, 55–65
  information structure, 67–83
  overview, 19
  purpose management, 41–53
  reader relationship, 23–39
  speaking, 191
  time allocated for, 14, 15, 20, 43
Prepositions, economical writing, 139–140
Prewriting (*See* Planning, five-stage writing)
Process knowledge, writing performance, 10, 11
Proofreading, 169–170
Prototype, draft as, 86–87, 96–97
Punctuation, revising stage, 167–173
Purpose management, planning stage, 41–53
  actions today, 53
  communication grid, 48–51
  exercise, 51–53
  importance of, 41–44
  ko and *mei* communication, 26, 46–47, 48–51
  long-term and short-term communication,
    47–51
  memo subject line replacement, 44–46
  planning stage overview, 19

"Quick and dirty" draft, 19, 85–93

Readability formulas, word choice, 156–159
Reader-based writing, 28–36, 98–99, 189–190

Reader relationship, planning stage, 23–39
    actions today, 38–39
    attitude, 29–32, 189–190
    circumstances, 32–35, 189–190
    communication-created community, 25–27
    exercise, 36–38
    importance of, 23–24
    knowledge, 35–36, 189–190
    personality, 27–29, 189–190
    planning stage overview, 19
Reading, and writing competence, 9, 10
Reinforcement, writing performance, 11
Remedies, management structure, 75–76
Reporter's checklist, 58
Resources for writing management, 60–62,
    193–196
Revising, five-stage writing, 109–173
    computer writing, 180
    economic writing, 135–143
    finishing writing, 167–173
    overview, 19–20
    paragraph management, 109–122
    sentence management, 112–118, 191–192
    sentence writing, 135–143
    speaking, 191–192
    subjects and verb management, 123–134
    tools for, 6, 110–112, 123–124
    word choice management, 145–165
    in writing process, 14, 15, 19–20
Rewriting (See Revising, five-stage writing)

Screen-based, online writing as, 181–184
Second wave communication, 3, 4
Sentence economy
    actions today, 143
    exercises, 140–143
    importance of, 135–137
    objectivity and common sense, 137–139
    overview, 19
    prepositions, 139–140
    relationship management, 112–118, 191–192
    revising for, 137–139
    revision tools, 6, 110–112, 123–124
    "which-hunt," 139
    (See also Revising, five-stage writing)
Sentence economy, revising stage, 135–143
Short-term communication, 47–51
Speaking management, 189–192
Speech and oral communication, 7–8, 189–192
Spelling, revising stage, 167–173
Structure of information (See Information
    structure, planning stage)

Styles, global communication, 186–187, 188
Subject and verb management, revising stage,
    123–134
    actions today, 133–134
    active or passive voice, 128–129
    exercise, 131–133
    hidden subjects, 124–125, 127–128
    hidden verbs, 126, 127–128
    modifiers, 129–131
    overview, 19
    tools for, 123–124
    (See also Revising, five-stage writing)

Thesauruses, as resource, 194
Thesis statement, 78
Third wave communication, 3–6
Time for writing, management of, 13–16, 20–21
Today, actions to take (See Actions today)
Tools for writing, 6, 110–112, 123–124
Training expectations, 9–11
Translate into English (See Word choice
    management, revising stage)
Transparency in writing, 9
"Turn signals," 112–118, 191–192
    (See also Paragraph management, revising
        stage)
12-step writing, 14–20
    (See also Five-stage writing)

Usage guides, as resource, 194

Verbs (See Subject and verb management,
    revising stage)

W/H questions, 58
Waves of change, communication, 3–6, 7
Web-based resources (See Internet)
What's in it for me (WIIFM) question, 45, 70–71
"Which-hunt," 139
WIIFM (What's in it for me) question, 45, 70–71
Win-win global communication, 186–187, 188
Word choice management, revising stage,
    145–165
    actions today, 164–165
    confusing or obfuscating language, 159–161
    exercises, 161–164
    importance of, 145–147
    IRS example, 147–149
    overview, 19
    readability formulas, 156–159
    reasons for choosing complexity, 153–155
    revision tools, 6, 110–112, 123–124

Word choice management, revising stage
   (*Cont.*):
   SEC guidelines, 155–159
   style checkers, 156–159
   word histories, 149–153
   (*See also* Revising, five-stage writing)
Write it now, drafts, 85–93
Writer, internal, 100–104
Writer's block, 10, 89
Writing guides, as resource, 195
Writing management overview, 1–21
   12-step writing, 14–20

Writing management overview (*Cont.*):
   actions today, 21
   communication in information society, 2–6
   discipline and practice, 12–13
   five-stage writing, 14–15, 17–20
   how to use this course, 11–12
   knowledge economy, 3–4, 6–8
   law of next action, 16–18
   lessons learned, 20–21
   time allocation, 13–16, 20–21
   training expectations, 9–11
   (*See also specific topics*)

ABOUT THE AUTHOR

Dr. Kenneth W. Davis is professor and former chair of English at Indiana University–Purdue University Indianapolis and president of Komei, Inc., a global training and consulting firm. His clients have included the Abu Dhabi National Oil Company, the Republic of Botswana, IBM, and the International Monetary Fund.

With more than 30 years experience as a business writer, editor, and trainer, Ken currently serves on the boards of directors of both the Association for Business Communication and the Association of Professional Communication Consultants. He lives in Indianapolis with his wife and business partner, Bette Davis.

Through speaking, training, and executive coaching, Ken helps people and organizations improve their chief value-producing activity: writing. Thousands of knowledge workers have profited from Ken's unique Manage Your Writing® method.

For more information on Ken's services—and to receive *Manage Your Writing* (a free e-book) and *Manage Your Writing This Week* (a free weekly writing tip)—go to http://www.ManageYourWriting.com.

FINAL EXAMINATION

THE McGRAW-HILL 36-HOUR COURSE IN BUSINESS WRITING AND COMMUNICATION

If you have completed your study of *The McGraw-Hill 36-Hour Course in Business Writing and Communication,* you should be prepared to take this final examination. It is a comprehensive test, consisting of 100 questions.

INSTRUCTIONS

1. You may treat this as an "open book" exam by consulting this and any other textbook. Or, you can reassure yourself that you have gained superior knowledge by taking the exam without reference to any other material.
2. Answer each of the test questions on the answer sheet provided at the end of the exam. For each question, write the letter of your choice on the answer blank that corresponds to the number of the question you are answering. Or, you may take the exam online at www.mcgraw-hill36-hourcourses.com.
3. All questions are multiple-choice, with four answers from which to choose. Always select the answer that represents in your mind the *best* among the choices.
4. Each correct answer is worth a point. A passing grade of 80 percent (80 correct answers) entitles you to receive a Certificate of Achievement. This handsome certificate, suitable for framing, attests to your proven knowledge of the contents of this course.
5. Carefully fill in your name and address in the spaces provided at the top of the answer sheet, remove the answer sheet from the book, and send it to:

Laura Libretti
McGraw-Hill
Professional Book Group
1333 Burr Ridge Parkway
Burr Ridge, IL 60527

1. Why is defining your community—your relationship with your reader(s)—the first step in the planning stage?

   a. It comes first alphabetically.

   b. It is represented by the *P* in the acronym PACK.

   c. All other planning decisions depend on it.

   d. It is the most difficult step.

2. Why is defining your purpose the second step in the planning stage?

   a. It should be done after defining your community—writer and reader(s).

   b. It should be done before collecting and organizing the content of your message.

   c. Both *a* and *b* are true.

   d. Neither *a* nor *b* is true.

3. Why is gathering information the third step in the planning stage?

   a. It should be done after defining your community—writer and reader(s)—and after defining your purpose.

   b. It should be done before organizing the content of your message.

   c. Both *a* and *b* are true.

   d. Neither *a* nor *b* is true.

4. Why is organizing information the fourth step in the planning stage?

   a. It should be done after defining your community, defining your purpose, and gathering your information.

   b. It should be done before drafting your message.

   c. Both *a* and *b* are true.

   d. Neither *a* nor *b* is true.

5. At what stage of the writing process should you decide the order in which you will present your main points?

   a. Managing

   b. Planning

   c. Drafting

   d. Revising

6. Which of the following shows the most effective use of "turn signals"?

   a. Capacity is more than 2.5 million barrels per day. Current production is much lower.

   b. Capacity is more than 2.5 million barrels per day, but current production is much lower.

    c. Capacity is more than 2.5 million barrels per day, and current production is much lower.

    d. Capacity is more than 2.5 million barrels per day because current production is much lower.

7. Which of the following sentences manages subjects and verbs most effectively?

    a. It seems probable that we will be unable to participate.

    b. We probably can't participate.

    c. Our participation will not be probable.

    d. There is a low probability that we will be able to participate.

8. Which of the following sentences is most economical without eliminating words that may carry important information?

    a. Textbook selection is accomplished through the use of a selection commission that consists of 10 members.

    b. Textbook selection is accomplished through the use of a 10-member selection commission.

    c. Textbooks are selected by a selection commission.

    d. Textbooks are selected by a 10-member commission.

9. Which of the following sentences uses words most effectively?

    a. The report is intended to provide information on a monthly basis to senior management and others as necessary.

    b. The report is meant to provide monthly information to senior management and others as necessary.

    c. The report is intended to provide information on a monthly basis to senior management and needed others.

    d. The report will get monthly information to senior managers and others.

10. Which of the following sentences is most conventional in spelling, punctuation, and mechanics?

    a. Please return the voltmeter to its case.

    b. Please return the voltmeter to it's case.

    c. Please return the voltmeter to its' case.

    d. None of the above answers uses conventional spelling.

11. Which of the following statements is most true?

    a. Community is necessary for communication.

    b. Communication is necessary for community.

    c. Both *a* and *b* are true.

    d. Neither *a* nor *b* is true.

12. Why do subject lines in memos and e-mail messages cause problems?
    a. They weren't invented for the reader(s) of the message.
    b. They are often vague.
    c. Both a and b are true.
    d. Neither a nor b is true.

13. Why should information gathering be done before drafting?
    a. To reduce interruptions during drafting
    b. To reduce the possibility of leaving out important information
    c. To give you the confidence to draft more easily
    d. All of the above

14. Why should organizing be done before drafting?
    a. To reduce interruptions during drafting
    b. To allow you to focus on the best order for the reader
    c. To turn the drafting job into a series of smaller jobs
    d. All of the above

15. At what stage of the writing process should you make sure a word is spelled correctly?
    a. Managing
    b. Planning
    c. Drafting
    d. Revising

16. Which of the following shows the most effective use of "turn signals"?
    a. The emirate produces liquefied natural gas. The emirate produces natural gas liquids.
    b. The emirate produces liquefied natural gas. However, the emirate produces natural gas liquids.
    c. The emirate produces liquefied natural gas and natural gas liquids.
    d. The emirate produces liquefied natural gas, but the emirate produces natural gas liquids.

17. Which of the following sentences manages subjects and verbs most effectively?
    a. We need to understand the strategy better.
    b. We have a need to gain a better understanding of the strategy.
    c. We need to gain a better understanding of the strategy.
    d. We have a need to understand the strategy better.

18. Which of the following sentences is most economical without eliminating words that may carry important information?

    a. All unopened packages should be returned to the dock on 41st Street.

    b. All unopened packages should be returned to the 41st Street dock.

    c. All packages that are not opened should be returned to the dock on 41st Street.

    d. All packages that are not opened should be returned to the dock that is on 41st Street.

19. Which of the following sentences uses words most effectively?

    a. As we examine our position in relation to supporting the fund drive, it seems that we will be unable to participate at the same level we did in 2004.

    b. We won't be able to give as much to the fund drive as we did in 2004.

    c. As we examine our position in relation to supporting the fund drive, it seems that we will be unable to contribute at the same level we did in 2004.

    d. As we review our position in relation to supporting the fund drive, it appears that we will be unable to participate at the same level we did in 2004.

20. Which of the following sentences is most conventional in spelling, punctuation, and mechanics?

    a. In his letter to us, he said that our proposal was alot of "hot air".

    b. In his letter to us, he said that our proposal was a lot of "hot air".

    c. In his letter to us, he said that our proposal was alot of "hot air."

    d. In his letter to us, he said that our proposal was a lot of "hot air."

21. In defining the community to which you and your reader(s) both belong, which of the following communities should you focus on?

    a. The largest possible community

    b. The smallest possible community

    c. The corporate community

    d. The international community

22. Using the subject line to define a message's purpose benefits whom?

    a. The writer because it encourages the writer to define his purpose

    b. The reader because it allows her to better screen and read the message

    c. Both the writer and the reader

    d. Neither the writer nor the reader

23. What kind(s) of questions are usually best to ask in an interview?

    a. Yes/no questions

    b. Multiple-choice questions

c. *Who, what, where, when, why,* and *how* questions

d. None of the above

24. Which of the following is a common difficulty with writing?

a. It requires converting linear thinking into nonlinear writing.

b. It requires converting nonlinear thinking into linear writing.

c. It requires converting static thinking into active writing.

d. None of the above.

25. At what stage of the writing process should you decide between two words with approximately the same meaning?

a. Managing

b. Planning

c. Drafting

d. Revising

26. Which of the following shows the most effective use of "turn signals"?

a. NGL is produced in two plants. One is on Das Island. One is at Ruwais.

b. NGL is produced in two plants. One is on Das Island, but one is at Ruwais.

c. NGL is produced in two plants. Therefore, one is on Das Island. One is at Ruwais.

d. NGL is produced in two plants: one is on Das Island and the other at Ruwais.

27. Which of the following sentences manages subjects and verbs most effectively?

a. I would like you to determine how such a process would be of benefit to us.

b. Please make a determination of how such a process would be of benefit to us.

c. Please determine how such a process would benefit us.

d. I would like you to make a determination of how such a process would benefit us.

28. Which of the following sentences is most economical without eliminating words that may carry important information?

a. Other factors that did not relate to an increased risk of cancer included . . .

b. Other factors unrelated to an increased risk of cancer included . . .

c. Other factors unrelated to an increased risk included . . .

d. Other factors unrelated to an increased cancer risk included . . .

29. Which of the following sentences uses words most effectively?

    a. The above information provides necessary information in evaluating the extent of opportunity available.

    b. The above information provides information necessary for the evaluation of the extent of opportunity available.

    c. This information tells us what we need to make a decision.

    d. This information is necessary for evaluating the extent of opportunity available.

30. Which of the following sentences is most conventional in spelling, punctuation, and mechanics?

    a. When will the new stationary be printed?

    b. When will the new stationery be printed?

    c. When will the new stationary be printted?

    d. When will the new stationery be printted?

31. In thinking about your audience, which of the following questions should you ask?

    a. How are my audience and I alike?

    b. How are my audience and I different?

    c. Both *a* and *b.*

    d. Neither *a* nor *b.*

32. Readers always want to know WIIFM. What do these letters stand for?

    a. Words, images, ideas, format, and mechanics

    b. What's in it for me?

    c. Whether included information facilitates metaphors

    d. Neither *a, b,* nor *c.*

33. The reporter's checklist can be valuable at what stage(s) of the writing process?

    a. The planning stage

    b. The revising stage

    c. Both *a* and *b*

    d. Neither *a* nor *b*

34. Which of the following is(are) characteristic(s) of "one stage" writers?

    a. They write in the order they think of things.

    b. They write in the most effective order for the reader.

    c. Both *a* and *b*

    d. Neither *a* nor *b*

35. At what stage of the writing process should you put sentences down on paper or on a computer screen?

    a. Managing

    b. Planning

    c. Drafting

    d. Revising

36. Which of the following shows the most effective use of "turn signals"?

    a. Some emirates have a corporate tax law, but it is applied only to foreign oil companies and foreign banks operating in those emirates.

    b. Some emirates have a corporate tax law. Therefore, it is applied only to foreign oil companies and foreign banks operating in those emirates.

    c. Some emirates have a corporate tax law. And it is applied only to foreign oil companies and foreign banks operating in those emirates.

    d. Some emirates have a corporate tax law, so it is applied only to foreign oil companies and foreign banks operating in those emirates.

37. Which of the following sentences manages subjects and verbs most effectively?

    a. It is difficult to control total expenses.

    b. There is a difficulty in the control of total expenses.

    c. Total expenses are difficult to control.

    d. It is the case that total expenses are difficult to control.

38. Which of the following sentences is most economical without eliminating words that may carry important information?

    a. The labels that are needed are rectangular in shape.

    b. The labels that are needed are rectangular.

    c. The needed labels are rectangular.

    d. The labels are rectangular.

39. ` Which of the following sentences uses words most effectively?

    a. After reviewing the data, we will talk with you about what happens next.

    b. After reviewing the data, we will be in contact with you to determine next steps as warranted.

    c. After reviewing the data, we will be in contact with you to determine next steps.

    d. After reviewing the data, we will contact you to determine next steps as warranted.

40. Which of the following sentences is most conventional in spelling, punctuation, and mechanics?

   a. The new tax law will effect our accounting system; it also will have a major affect on our tax flow.

   b. The new tax law will effect our accounting system; it also will have a major effect on our tax flow.

   c. The new tax law will affect our accounting system; it also will have a major affect on our tax flow.

   d. The new tax law will affect our accounting system; it also will have a major effect on our tax flow.

41. When you and your reader have different personality types, which of the following best expresses what you should do?

   a. Simply be yourself, in the confidence that your reader will be able to adjust.

   b. Consider both your personality type and your reader's, and adjust as necessary to your reader's personality.

   c. Ignore personality differences; they are unimportant in business communication.

   d. Find common ground with your reader in a third personality type.

42. All communication has both *ko* and *mei* functions. What do those root words mean?

   a. Oral and written

   b. Long term and short term

   c. Communication and community

   d. Together and change

43. The four pairs of questions for information gathering are based on which of the following sets of words?

   a. Personality, attitude(s), circumstances, knowledge

   b. Same/different, whole/parts, time/space, cause/effect

   c. *Ko* and *mei*

   d. None of the above

44. Should formal outlines be used at the planning stage?

   a. Yes; they always should be used.

   b. No; they never should be used.

   c. They should be used only if they are useful to the writer.

   d. They should be used only when writing speeches.

45. At what stage of the writing process should you determine the purpose of your writing?

   a. Managing

   b. Planning

   c. Drafting

   d. Revising

46. Which of the following shows the most effective use of "turn signals"?

   a. The meeting was very beneficial, but new subjects were discussed.

   b. The meeting was very beneficial, so new subjects were discussed.

   c. The meeting was very beneficial because new subjects were discussed.

   d. The meeting was very beneficial; however, new subjects were discussed.

47. Which of the following sentences manages subjects and verbs most effectively?

   a. It is my opinion that market segmentation issues are clear.

   b. It is my opinion that there is clarity in market segmentation issues.

   c. I believe that there is clarity in market segmentation issues.

   d. I believe that market segmentation issues are clear.

48. Which of the following sentences is most economical without eliminating words that may carry important information?

   a. There are several projects that are successful that use volunteers.

   b. There are several successful projects that use volunteers.

   c. Several successful projects use volunteers.

   d. Several projects that are successful use volunteers.

49. Which of the following sentences uses words most effectively?

   a. We did not attempt to estimate the potential negative effect on our business.

   b. We did not attempt to estimate the potential negative impact on our business.

   c. We did not attempt to calculate the potential negative effect on our business.

   d. We did not try to estimate the potential harm to our business.

50. Which of the following sentences is most conventional in spelling, punctuation, and mechanics?

   a. Abu Dhabi is the capitol and principle city of the United Arab Emirates.

   b. Abu Dhabi is the capitol and principal city of the United Arab Emirates.

   c. Abu Dhabi is the capital and principle city of the United Arab Emirates.

   d. Abu Dhabi is the capital and principal city of the United Arab Emirates.

51. If you're a "feeler" writing to a "thinker," which of the following should you do?

    a. Avoid being overly sentimental.

    b. Make sure that you support your opinions logically.

    c. Make your thinking process clear.

    d. All of the above.

52. Most pieces of communication have what function?

    a. A community-building function

    b. A change function

    c. Both a and b

    d. Neither a nor b

53. Which of the following is *not* good advice for interviewing?

    a. Prepare for the interview by reading and by listing questions.

    b. Don't be distracted from your list of questions by the interviewee's responses.

    c. Ask basic W/H questions.

    d. Write down what you've learned as soon as possible.

54. Unless you have a good reason for doing otherwise, how should routine requests for information begin?

    a. With background information

    b. With the request itself, phrased as a question if possible

    c. With friendly, personal information

    d. With the reason for the request

55. At what stage of the writing process should you allocate time for the other stages in the process?

    a. Managing

    b. Planning

    c. Drafting

    d. Revising

56. Which of the following shows the most effective use of "turn signals"?

    a. The subcommittee report did not arrive in time. It had to be mailed to participants later.

    b. The subcommittee report did not arrive in time, but it had to be mailed to participants later.

    c. The subcommittee report did not arrive in time, and it had to be mailed to participants later.

d. The subcommittee report did not arrive in time, so it had to be mailed to participants later.

57. Which of the following sentences manages subjects and verbs most effectively?

   a. Currently, there is no defined career development process within headquarters.

   b. Currently, headquarters has no defined career development process.

   c. There is currently no defined career development process within headquarters.

   d. At the current time, there is no defined career development process within headquarters.

58. Which of the following sentences is most economical without eliminating words that may carry important information?

   a. Please submit a report each week that lists all customer complaints.

   b. Please submit a report listing all customer complaints.

   c. Please submit a weekly report listing all customer complaints.

   d. Please submit a report each week listing all customer complaints.

59. Which of the following sentences uses words most effectively?

   a. If you agree, please contact the Foundation and advise them that you are our company's representative and that all future correspondence should be directed to you.

   b. If you agree, please tell the Foundation that you are our representative and ask them to send all mail to you.

   c. If you agree, please contact the Foundation and tell them that you are our company's representative and that all future correspondence should be sent to you.

   d. If you agree, please contact the Foundation and tell them that you are our company's representative and request that they direct all future correspondence to you.

60. Which of the following sentences is most conventional in spelling, punctuation, and mechanics?

   a. She has already read your letter and says your suggestion is alright with her.

   b. She has already read your letter and says your suggestion is all right with her.

   c. She has all ready read your letter and says your suggestion is alright with her.

   d. She has all ready read your letter and says your suggestion is all right with her.

61. Which of the following statements about attitudes is most true?

    a. Similarities and differences between your attitude and that of your audience should be considered at the planning stage.

    b. Consideration of similarities and differences between your attitude and that of your audience should be postponed until the revision stage.

    c. Consideration of attitudes should not enter into the business writing process.

    d. None of the above.

62. Which of the following is probably *not* an example of "conversation" communication as defined in this book?

    a. A birthday card

    b. A discussion, over lunch, of your children's activities

    c. A corporate mission statement

    d. A question about the reader's family at the beginning of a business e-mail message

63. Which of these statements about information on the Web is most true?

    a. Web-based information is almost always accurate.

    b. Web-based information is almost always inaccurate.

    c. Web-based information can be accurate or inaccurate, so it should be read and used critically.

    d. Web-based information can be accurate or inaccurate, so it should not be used.

64. Unless you have a good reason for doing otherwise, how should claims begin?

    a. With background information

    b. With the request itself, phrased as a question if possible

    c. With friendly, personal information

    d. With a statement of the problem

65. At what stage of the writing process should you get a general idea of how to start and end the piece of writing?

    a. Managing

    b. Planning

    c. Drafting

    d. Revising

66. Which of the following shows the most effective use of "turn signals"?

    a. The report will cover traditional uses of LPG. It will cover use of LPG as an alternative transport fuel.

    b. The report will cover both traditional uses of LPG and its use as an alternative transport fuel.

    c. The report will cover traditional uses of LPG. However, it will cover uses of LPG as an alternative transport fuel.

    d. The report will cover traditional uses of LPG, but it will cover its uses as an alternative transport fuel.

67. Which of the following sentences manages subjects and verbs most effectively?

    a. It is my hope that you will submit a proposal.

    b. I hope you will submit a proposal.

    c. Your submission of a proposal is my hope.

    d. I hope you will make a proposal submission.

68. Which of the following sentences is most economical without eliminating words that may carry important information?

    a. The agency will prepare a catalogue of the skills that each staff member possesses.

    b. The agency will catalogue each staff member's skills.

    c. The agency will prepare a catalogue of the skills of each staff member.

    d. The agency will prepare a catalogue of skills.

69. Which of the following sentences uses words most effectively?

    a. I would like for you to investigate the feasibility of managing the timely clearance of priority items from your area.

    b. I would like for you to look into the feasibility of managing the timely clearance of priority items from your area.

    c. Please investigate the feasibility of managing the timely clearance of priority items from your area.

    d. Please look into how you can clear priority items on time.

70. Which of the following sentences is most conventional in spelling, punctuation, and mechanics?

    a. I'm sure you've perceived the new title occuring after my name.

    b. I'm sure you've perceived the new title occurring after my name.

    c. I'm sure you've percieved the new title occuring after my name.

    d. I'm sure you've percieved the new title occurring after my name.

71. Which of the following statements about the Maslow hierarchy of needs is most true?

    a. It is a handy checklist of punctuation rules.

    b. It can help you to assess how your writing can fill a need for your reader.

    c. It describes the five needed stages in the writing process.

    d. None of the above.

72. Which of the following is probably *not* an example of "correspondence" communication as defined in this book?

    a. A birthday card

    b. A telephone call to order office supplies

    c. An e-mail message to order office supplies

    d. A faxed order for office supplies

73. Which of the following is *not* good advice for brainstorming in writing?

    a. Jot down ideas as quickly as you can.

    b. Don't be concerned about the order ideas are in.

    c. List only those ideas that you're sure you'll use in the piece of writing.

    d. Answers *a, b,* and *c* are all good advice.

74. Unless you have a good reason for doing otherwise, how should good-news responses begin?

    a. With background information

    b. With the good news

    c. With friendly, personal information

    d. With any qualifications about the good news

75. At what stage of the writing process should you review a paragraph to see if it has enough transition words?

    a. Managing

    b. Planning

    c. Drafting

    d. Revising

76. Which of the following shows the most effective use of "turn signals"?

    a. The course will examine global supply and demand balances. The course will examine regional supply and demand balances.

    b. The course will examine global supply and demand balances, but it will examine regional supply and demand balances.

    c. The course will examine global supply and demand balances. The course will also examine regional supply and demand balances.

    d. The course will examine global and regional supply and demand balances.

77. Which of the following sentences manages subjects and verbs most effectively?

    a. The course will examine global supply and demand balances.

    b. The course will make an examination of global supply and demand balances.

    c. An examination of global supply and demand balances will be made by the course.

    d. There will be in the course an examination of global supply and demand balances.

78. Which of the following sentences is most economical without eliminating words that may carry important information?

    a. The chairman will make a speech on the problems in marketing that the company has encountered.

    b. The chairman will speak on the problems in marketing that the company has encountered.

    c. The chairman will make a speech on the problems in marketing encountered by the company.

    d. The chairman will speak on the company's marketing problems.

79. Which of the following sentences uses words most effectively?

    a. The chairman will present a speech on the difficulties in marketing that the company has encountered.

    b. The chairman will speak on the difficulties in marketing that the company has encountered.

    c. The chairman will make a speech on the problems in marketing encountered by the company.

    d. The chairman will speak on the company's marketing problems.

80. Which of the following sentences is most conventional in spelling, punctuation, and mechanics?

    a. In retracing his path, the courier was worryed that he might have omitted something.

    b. In retracing his path, the courier was worried that he might have omitted something.

    c. In retraceing his path, the courier was worryed that he might have omited something.

    d. In retraceing his path, the courier was worried that he might have omited something.

81. In visualizing your reader, which of the following statements is most true?

    a. You should visualize your reader at his best.

    b. You should visualize your reader at his worst.

    c. You should visualize your reader reading and reacting to your message.

    d. You should focus on your reader's face.

82. Which of the following is probably *not* an example of "covenant" communication as defined in this book?

    a. A mission statement

    b. An oral story of your company's founding

    c. A corporate privacy policy

    d. A profit-and-loss statement for the month

83. Which of the following statements about mind-mapping is true?

    a. A mind map should include only the information you'll use in the piece of writing.

    b. An mind map should map information in the order in which it will be used in the piece of writing.

    c. An effective mind map can be done only by computer.

    d. None of these statements is true.

84. Unless you have a good reason for doing otherwise, how should bad-news responses begin?

    a. With background information

    b. With the bad news

    c. With an acknowledgment of the request

    d. With any qualifications about the bad news

85. At what stage of the writing process should you get an initial sense of your audience?

    a. Managing

    b. Planning

    c. Drafting

    d. Revising

86. Which of the following shows the most effective use of "turn signals"?

    a. The February meeting was canceled. Many participants would be unable to attend.

    b. The February meeting was canceled, and many participants would be unable to attend.

      c. The February meeting was canceled, but many participants would be unable to attend.

      d. The February meeting was canceled because many participants would be unable to attend.

87. Which of the following sentences manages subjects and verbs most effectively?

      a. The April meeting was canceled by action of the director.

      b. The cancellation of the April meeting was made by the director.

      c. The director declared the April meeting canceled.

      d. The director canceled the April meeting.

88. Which of the following sentences is most economical without eliminating words that may carry important information?

      a. The costs of implementation will be offset by savings in time.

      b. The implementation costs will be offset by time savings.

      c. The costs of implementation will be offset by time savings.

      d. The implementation costs will be offset by savings in time.

89. Which of the following sentences uses words most effectively?

      a. The Girls' State Basketball Tournament wherein the souvenir program is distributed commands an annual attendance of approximately 95,000 people.

      b. The Girls' State Basketball Tournament, where the souvenir program is distributed, draws about 95,000 people each year.

      c. The Girls' State Basketball Tournament wherein the souvenir program is distributed draws an attendance of approximately 95,000 people annually.

      d. The Girls' State Basketball Tournament, where the souvenir program is distributed, commands an annual attendance of about 95,000 people.

90. Which of the following sentences is most conventional in spelling, punctuation, and mechanics?

      a. The flag is red, green, white, and black.

      b. The flag is red, green, white and black.

      c. Both *a* and *b* are conventional.

      d. Neither *a* nor *b* is conventional.

91. Which of the following best expresses the meaning of the acronym COIK?

      a. COIK material will be understandable by the reader only if the reader already knows it.

      b. COIK material is adjusted to the four elements of the reader's personality.

    c. COIK material considers the reader's circumstances, opportunities, intelligence, and knowledge.

    d. None of the above.

92. Which of the following is probably *not* an example of "conception" communication as defined in this book?

    a. A speech by a CEO projecting five-year goals for the company

    b. A corporate vision statement

    c. A corporate history

    d. A written timeline of goals for the next 10 years

93. Any writing you do at the information-gathering stage should have which of the following characteristics?

    a. It should be spelled and punctuated carefully.

    b. It should be based on your definitions of audience and purpose for the writing job.

    c. It should be organized carefully.

    d. All of the above.

94. Which of the following is *not* a feature of indirect persuasion?

    a. It begins with a clear statement of your position.

    b. It begins with a clear statement of the problem.

    c. It acknowledges and clearly states your opponents' position(s).

    d. It describes the circumstances in which your opponents' position is correct.

95. At what stage of the writing process should you collect any information you need for the writing?

    a. Managing

    b. Planning

    c. Drafting

    d. Revising

96. Which of the following shows the most effective use of "turn signals"?

    a. The writing process has five stages. They are managing, planning, drafting, breaking, and revising.

    b. The writing process has five stages: managing, planning, drafting, breaking, and revising.

    c. The writing process has five stages. But they are managing, planning, drafting, breaking, and revising.

     d. The writing process has five stages. Therefore, they are managing, plan-
     ning, drafting, breaking, and revising.

97. Which of the following sentences manages subjects and verbs most effectively?
     a. The writing process has five stages.
     b. There are five stages in the writing process.
     c. It is the case that the writing process has five stages.
     d. It is the case that there are five stages in the writing process.

98. Which of the following sentences is most economical without eliminating
words that may carry important information?
     a. The process of writing has five (5) stages.
     b. The writing process has five (5) stages.
     c. The writing process has five stages.
     d. The process of writing has five stages.

99. Which of the following sentences uses words most effectively?
     a. The process of written composition possesses five successive stages.
     b. The process of written composition has five stages.
     c. The writing process has five stages.
     d. The process of written composition possesses five stages.

100. Which of the following sentences is most conventional in spelling, punctuation,
and mechanics?
     a. Did she complete the form marked "Secret"?
     b. Did she complete the form marked "Secret?"
     c. "Where do we go from here?" he asked.
     d. Both *a* and *c* are correct.

Name _____

Address _____

City _____ State _____ Zip _____

FINAL EXAMINATION ANSWER SHEET: THE McGRAW-HILL 36-HOUR COURSE IN BUSINESS WRITING AND COMMUNICATION

See instructions on page E-1 of the Final Examination.

1. _____	21. _____	41. _____	61. _____	81. _____
2. _____	22. _____	42. _____	62. _____	82. _____
3. _____	23. _____	43. _____	63. _____	83. _____
4. _____	24. _____	44. _____	64. _____	84. _____
5. _____	25. _____	45. _____	65. _____	85. _____
6. _____	26. _____	46. _____	66. _____	86. _____
7. _____	27. _____	47. _____	67. _____	87. _____
8. _____	28. _____	48. _____	68. _____	88. _____
9. _____	29. _____	49. _____	69. _____	89. _____
10. _____	30. _____	50. _____	70. _____	90. _____
11. _____	31. _____	51. _____	71. _____	91. _____
12. _____	32. _____	52. _____	72. _____	92. _____
13. _____	33. _____	53. _____	73. _____	93. _____
14. _____	34. _____	54. _____	74. _____	94. _____
15. _____	35. _____	55. _____	75. _____	95. _____
16. _____	36. _____	56. _____	76. _____	96. _____
17. _____	37. _____	57. _____	77. _____	97. _____
18. _____	38. _____	58. _____	78. _____	98. _____
19. _____	39. _____	59. _____	79. _____	99. _____
20. _____	40. _____	60. _____	80. _____	100. _____